THE POETRY OF LIFE

THE POETRY OF LIFE

AND THE LIFE OF POETRY

ESSAYS AND REVIEWS

BY DAVID MASON

STORY LINE PRESS
2000

Published by Story Line Press, Three Oaks Farm, PO Box 1240, Ashland, OR 97520-0055
www.storylinepress.com

This publication was made possible thanks in part to the generous support of the Nicholas Roerich Museum, the Andrew W. Mellon Foundation, the National Endowment for the Arts, and our individual contributors.

Book design by Lysa McDowell
Cover Oil Painting, "Manzanita" © Janis Gabriel

Library of Congress Cataloging-in-Publication Data

Mason, David, 1954–
    The poetry of life and the life of poetry: essays and reviews / by David Mason.
    p. cm.
ISBN 1-885266-80-4 (pbk:alk. paper)
    1. Poetry—Book reviews. 2. English poetry—History and criticism. 3. American poetry—History and criticism. I. Title.

PS3563.A7879P642000
821'.91409—dc21   *99-048539*

ACKNOWLEDGEMENTS

Most of these essays have been revised yet again since their first appearance, often on the advice of friends. Dana Gioia, a valued friend for many years, has been particularly helpful. I have also received good suggestions from R. S. Gwynn and others, including my publisher, Robert McDowell. Much of this work first appeared in *The Hudson Review*, where Frederick Morgan and Paula Deitz have been the most trusting guides imaginable, and Ron Koury has corrected many small errors. I should also like to thank George Core of *The Sewanee Review*, Robert McPhillips of *Verse*, Gerry Cambridge of *The Dark Horse*, Daniel Tynan who commissioned the piece on J.V. Cunningham, Felix and Selma Stefanile of *Sparrow*, Jay and Martha Meek of *North Dakota Quarterly*, the editorial board of *The Cumberland Poetry Review*, Professor Francesco Binni in Rome, who asked for an essay about New Formalism, Nicholas Jenkins of the W. H. Auden Society and Peter van de Kamp, whose Kerry International Summer School provided me a forum in which to shape my thinking about Irish and American writers. Daniel Albright and Anthony Hecht gave wise counsel when I wrote about W. H. Auden. Betty Kucera and Jasmine Smith helped with the typescript. Moorhead State University encouraged me to pursue my work as a poet-critic, as did The Colorado College, and there are other helpful friends and colleagues too numerous to list. The greatest debt I owe, of course, is acknowledged in the book's dedication.

For Annie, with love

CONTENTS

PREFACE

Growing up in the far northwestern corner of the United States, I usually assumed that culture and the arts existed elsewhere — Chicago or New York or Europe. In my youthful and myopic vision, America east of the Mississippi seemed one great urban monolith, like the photos I had seen of Manhattan, and I thought I lived in a part of the world that, somehow, didn't count for much. I had plenty to distract me in the woods and lakes, the Cascade Mountains, the murky tides of the Puget Sound. Yet, though I knew adults whose primary concerns were fishing and lumbering, most of my parents' friends led active intellectual lives. Some were professors, though not English professors. Some were lawyers, doctors, engineers. I was privileged to hear their talk, which was full not only of politics, but also of the latest books they had read, often discussed with infectious gusto. These were people who had come from those other cities I knew so little about, most of them making a fresh start out west in the boom years after World War II. The culture they brought with them was never forced upon me, but I felt myself drawn to it in the same way that I was drawn to nature. I listened to them at the dinner table, or out on summer lawns, and I wanted to join in the conversation.

I remember two of the books that influenced me in those early days. One was Theodore Roethke's *I Am! Says the Lamb*. On its blue dustjacket I read that the poet lived in Seattle. This astonished me. A poet in Seattle! How could it be true? Little did I know that there were several poets in Seattle at various times, from Elizabeth Bishop to Carolyn Kizer, Richard Hugo to David Wagoner. It would be years before I knew that I had tramped through some of the same hills and mountains where Gary Snyder had lived.

Still, I didn't quite trust the writers of my region until I picked up Oscar Williams' *Pocket Book of Modern Verse,* where I found poets of the west like Robinson Jeffers and J.V. Cunningham rubbing shoulders with Walt Whitman, Dylan Thomas and Edna St. Vincent Millay. Robert Frost was a transplanted Californian, and Ezra Pound hailed from Hailey, Idaho. I began to understand, or think I did, that there was a larger community of words to which all writers belonged, that there were sometimes very disparate voices in this community, but that poems of great beauty and excitement came from a wide variety of places and in many forms.

As I slowly, painfully became a writer, I often felt excluded from the larger cultural debate—the one going on in the magazines and journals I read—because I was provincial, and therefore could have nothing to say that would interest more sophisticated minds. Sometimes I even hated this thing called culture, preferring the mountains to any museum, without knowing that such bifurcation has often appeared in American life and letters. There was nothing orderly or systematic in my reading; my own career as a professor got started rather late, as much through desperation and happenstance as anything else. I remember reading Tolstoy and Melville while I worked in Alaska, unloading crab and shrimp boats, and later I hitchhiked for seven months in Britain, Ireland and Spain, where I read more Tolstoy, Oscar Wilde, Malcolm Lowry and others. These were among the most powerful reading experiences in my life. In fact, when I got out of college I swore I would never set foot on a campus again because I did not want others to dictate what I read.

For most of the decade of my twenties, I lived away from the academic world. There were two years as a gardener and estate caretaker in Upstate New York, thirteen months living in a small Greek village, where I fell in love with the great work of Homer, and moderns like Seferis and Cavafy. A year working for a film company back in the U.S. brought me my first substantial income as a writer. I thought I was a novelist, and still have four failed novels written in my twenties, draft upon draft packed away in boxes like mementos of another life. When the film company went bust, I spent several more years as a gardener, house painter, odd-job man, all the while lugging the terrible weight of my own failure. I needed to make a living, had tired of manual labor, and was given a chance by The Colorado College to discover that I enjoyed teaching. Over the years, I have found teaching to be extraordinarily demanding, yet my efforts in the classroom have much in common with my efforts to write criticism. I want to convey a passion for learning matched by an interest in life.

Criticism is creative to the extent that it is stubbornly independent. My purpose in these essays and reviews has been to stand as an individual, admitting my allegiances and dislikes when I can, while trying to convey my love of reading, particularly of poetry, to others. Those familiar with contemporary poetry criticism will no doubt see how indebted I am to Dana Gioia's book, *Can Poetry Matter?* Several of the pieces here make specific reference to his work. I begin by assuming that poetry does matter, often more than we realize, but that poets ought to hold themselves to higher standards than they sometimes do. In the title essay, I treat the idea of poetry broadly, finding it in prose, perhaps even in the lived life, as well as in verse. But I move next to appreciations of Auden, for whom poetry was "a game of knowledge," recognizing the pleasures of artifice as much as the urgency of felt experience. By looking at figures such as Homer, Tennyson, Frost, Heaney and Sexton, I can say something about the poet's relation to the larger world, and of course I also want to write about poets of my own generation as well. There are other preoccupations in the book, but I should at least note that I end where I began, by writing on a fine poet of the west coast, John Haines.

In all of these pieces I ask simple questions: "Why should I care about this or that writer? Why does this work deserve attention? What does it have to do with the life we are living now?" I have in mind that audience of grown-ups arguing about books even while they discuss their divorces, the latest political tremors or a new movie coming to town. Poetry ought to serve them at least as much as it serves poets and critics, and I do not mean to use the idea of service in the simplistic terms of social acquiescence. The chief advantage of an active intellectual life lies in being taken out of ourselves, listening to voices other than our own.

So what characterizes the historical moment in which we find ourselves regarding the practice of poetry? I sense an almost Elizabethan ferment, an expansion and rediscovery of the possibilities of the English language, which is clearly, for better and worse, a global cultural force. But I do not see any commanding figure who, like Shakespeare, can marshall the full potential of the art. Instead it seems we have an age of smaller talents, some of them extremely fine. In America we have lately had a tussle called "the poetry wars," a series of arguments often couched in angry political terms. By co-editing (with Mark Jarman) an anthology called *Rebel Angels: 25 Poets of the New Formalism,* I have played a small part in this ramshackle debate. But the terms of the debate have often been so confused, so full of rancor, that its implications remain far from clear. Readers of the present volume will, I hope, notice my affection for the energy and brilliance of the best work of Eliot, Pound, Williams, Stevens and other modernists, as well as for relative mavericks like J.V. Cunningham and Thomas McGrath. Of course the political beliefs of these writers are extremely important, sometimes disturbing, even despicable, but they are not the whole story. Poetry addresses other kinds of experience too.

Now, long after the energies of modernism have waned, I have felt some disappointment with what has emerged to replace it. My only recourse as a critic has been to listen, as it were, to my own heart and discover where my affection lay. As I read contemporary poetry, I have found a great deal of self-indulgence. Though I have nothing against the personal in art, I do want it transformed, made into something beyond an advertisement for the self. I often saw a movement away from beautiful or memorable language, a slackening of poetic energies to the point where most prose held my interest more readily than verse. Those contemporary poets who attempted to be visionary often did so in a language that poorly served their ideas — Ginsberg's "Howl" now seems to me a crashing bore, whatever its historical interest — and most other poets appeared to have no vision at all, but to have acquiesced in a long, steady drift toward lackadaisical prose. I remember a time in the 1970s and 80s when two poets I greatly admired, Anthony Hecht and Richard Wilbur, were regularly condemned in political terms because they emphasized the artifice in their art, and this condemnation seemed to me gravely mistaken.

Though I strongly dislike the term "New Formalism," which has been foisted on some recent poets, and which Jarman and I felt compelled to use in the subtitle of our anthology, I greatly admire a number of the writers associated with the movement, and I have tried to write sensibly about them here. I like this effort to embrace the oldest ideas about the poet (maker as well as seer) without losing contemporary relevance. The best of the New Formalists, like the best of the old, have done just that, retaining the right to use any poetic form they choose, while exploring a variety of subjects. What is new in poetry becomes an addition to tradition rather than a replacement of it. As Wallace Stevens so aptly put it, "One cannot spend one's time in being modern when there are so many more important things to be." Poets serve an art as well as a tribe or themselves as individuals, and that art cannot escape the nature of its medium, language, any more than it can deny the many traditions that feed the language. We must be able to ask who has made the most memorable, the most truthful poems of our time; otherwise, the art disintegrates into mere careerism. Here, it seems, the critic has a responsibility to join the discussion, as I have tried to do.

Reading contemporary poetry, it is possible to become cynical. So little of it demands to be remembered. Surely this has always been true, but that should not keep us from talking about it. I want not only to defend my sort of poetry, but to press forgotten questions—frequently on aesthetic matters—which of course cannot entirely be distinguished from all the other forces defining us as human beings. Do not expect any systematic answers—not from a reader as wayward and easily distracted as I. But I will at least assert that the Greeks had it fundamentally right: poetry is making, construction, fabrication. It is the most active engagement with experience possible through the medium of words. When we talk about it, we must talk not only about language, but also about experience in the broadest terms. Whatever form they take, the poems I love most also convey the pleasure of something well made, constructed, fabricated, and I believe that poets are creatures of such love, as well as their quarrels with the world.

THE POETRY OF LIFE
AND THE LIFE OF POETRY

It's like a book, I think, this bloomin' world....
                              — Rudyard Kipling

1. FORMS OF MEMORY

I owe my existence to the Japanese Imperial Army. Not in the way you might be guessing — the incident I am about to relate happened a decade before I was born, and my mother was safely tucked away in a California college for women.

It happened to my father at twenty-four, a red-haired Naval lieutenant on the bridge of a destroyer, the USS *Terry*, patrolling the waters off Iwo Jima. You know about the famous battle there, five weeks of the bloodiest conflict imaginable — unimaginable, in fact, the stories numbing a listener, the storytellers so physically or psychologically wounded that sometimes they can hardly bear their own survival. Compared to the Marines on the island, who often fought hand-to-hand against the Japanese, my father's position at sea was, I suppose, relatively safe. He never spoke of this when I was growing up. Now in his seventies, he tells the story as if it can't be suppressed any longer, as if he too can't believe he survived.

In daytime the destroyers usually lay off the southeast shore of Iwo Jima, bombarding targets radioed to them by Marine spotters. On this particular night they were sent to protect supply ships moving away from the island. The crew, at battle stations all night, had evaded a torpedo dropped from one of the Japanese planes that scouted them. As dawn came, the destroyers were ordered back to their daytime stations. While the Captain and crew tried to sleep, my father, Officer of the Deck, took the ship down the northeast side of the island several miles from shore.

He couldn't have known the enemy had hidden heavy artillery in caves on the island. These were British coastal guns captured at Singapore, mounted on rails so they could be wheeled out, fired, and wheeled back into their caves before invaders detected their location. Years later I listened to my father converse with a man who had been an artillery officer in the Canadian Army. This friend described the noise made by these big British guns, and my father said, "I know that noise. I've been shot at by them."

The first shells fired from the island at the *Terry* exploded in huge geysers just off the bow. My father ordered a zigzag course away from the island and wakened the Captain, who then took charge as my father ran to his post on the gun-director turret. He had hardly reached it when they were hit—WHAM—smack in the middle of the ship. All electrical circuits went out at once and the five-inch guns were left to fire at the shore as best they could.

"Blood all over the place," my father said. He was okay, but he felt stunned and helpless. Everywhere there were young boys killed or missing body parts. As if God had made a fist and brought it down amidships. A lot of boys had been alive, and suddenly they were in pieces. The dying or seriously wounded were more than the doctor and the one uninjured corpsman could handle. The engine rooms were flooded and the *Terry* lay dead in the water until other ships came to take her in tow.

The memory of dead and wounded boys has never left my father; it may have contributed to his decision after the war to become a doctor. He could not talk about it for years. He mistrusted the words, or the impact they might have on him or us if he tried to describe it all, especially his own questions about whether he had set the ship on the best course that morning. But the truth is that nobody had known about the hidden guns.

For the *Terry* the battle of Iwo Jima had ended. They were going home, which meant they would miss the dreaded invasion of Japan. Not all of them made it, however. My father's Gunnery Officer friend received a transfer to another destroyer headed for Okinawa. He remembers the young man's grief at the news; as his eyes filled with tears he had said, "I know I'll never see my wife again."

Whenever I hear that part of the story I think of the movies. You know what will happen next. The guy who takes out the photo of his wife or girlfriend is always the guy who gets killed in the next battle. We've watched it happen so often that we can hardly believe it any more. But life is sometimes full of clichés. You don't have to believe in fate to say that so-and-so was fated to die in such and such a way. Even as I write this I wonder: Am I telling you the story, or merely transcribing a version of some war story that has happened many times over? Do I give form to the tale, or do I uncover a form that is already there? Fated or not, this young officer was killed instantly by a *kamikaze* when it crashed into the bridge of his new ship.

My father and the *Terry* were spared the *kamikazes*. They limped home to the United States for a period of recovery. At a dance near San Francisco my father and mother met — so you can see how I owe my existence to the Japanese Imperial Army. If they had not captured the British guns at Singapore and shipped them to Iwo Jima with its ant farm of caves and opened fire on the USS *Terry*, my brothers and I would never have been born.

This story, it often seems to me, has an inherent form; the teller only uncovers it. We say that life is full of ironies, which we discover by looking back, even looking back only a moment or two. But do we live the plots of stories already told? Do the seasons and planets rhyme? Perhaps these are idle questions. Everyone knows that life is formless and that art is not. Even the most chaotic painting has a frame around it, but who are we to say that birth and death are the frame around our lives? We assume that life is chaos. Our usual metaphors are a wilderness, a wind-tossed sea, a jungle with or without sidewalks. And so it seems. We see through a glass, darkly. We call art, as Robert Frost called poetry, "a momentary stay against confusion."

But to say that we do not always perceive a form is not proof that no form exists. Our greatest pleasures often derive from form — the feeling of connection, completion, touch. It seems that the mind naturally rejects formlessness. As John Frederick Nims has written, "The word *form* has a variety of meanings, some of them antipodal. For the philosophers *forma* can mean *soul* the in*form*ing principle that animates whatever is alive and organizes whatever is not. But for most writers *form* is more likely to mean *body* than *soul*...." Whether we create form or merely perceive its immanence in nature, or both, I cannot say. But I can at least explore some of those moments when life seems to have a shape, when it seems poetic, and compare them to the life of poetry, the routine devotion to its pleasures.

I have sometimes felt that I was part of a story, and that I had a sacred duty to transcribe as much of it as I could. My story has something to do with my father's war. In 1974 I unloaded fishing boats for six months in Dutch Harbor, Alaska, which, as it happens, had been bombed by the Japanese in World War II. Dutch Harbor was still a little-known outpost, not quite halfway out the Aleutian Chain. When I lived there it was an empty place, ghostly, its weather usually dreary like a sodden blanket. The hills were utterly bare, like Hebridean moors, and one could see spent volcanoes on the island of Unalaska. Everywhere there were empty buildings: Quonset huts and old wooden barracks weathered silver. There were broken concrete bunkers, rusty trucks half-buried on the beaches, miles of oxidized copper wire running through the weedy tundra. These were the ruins of a World War II military base. I have known several men who served there during the war. They shudder when they recall the horizontal rain, the steady boredom, the horror of Attu—a smaller Iwo Jima—and not one of them has ever expressed to me a desire to return to that place.

My own memories are not so hellish, and with good reason. In 1974 we had finished our latest war and had only Watergate to worry about. But I do remember the ruins: the old prison camp, the officers' quarters. Dutch Harbor was a sort of garbage dump of World War II, a scavenger's paradise. I thought of it as my essential landscape—the desolate home of all literal and figurative war babies, the off-center eye of history's storm.

Derek Walcott, who grew up on another isolated island far to the south, has said that "The sigh of history rises over ruins, not over landscapes...." That is not entirely true. Sometimes the landscape is the ruined temple. Sometimes it is the battlefield. In South Dakota, for example, you can still see the shallow ravine at Wounded Knee where the Seventh Cavalry slaughtered three hundred Sioux. There is a wooden sign on which the word "Battle" has been replaced by the word "Massacre." There is a graveyard with a small monument. But the landscape is haunted too. The story lives in the grass and the lay of the land.

I felt that way about Dutch Harbor. Walking far from the ghost town of old barracks, I still felt the presence of history like some aboriginal songline. Unalaska's Church of the Holy Ascension attests to the Russian conquerors and their God, but so does the distant, snowy volcano with its Russian name. It wasn't only the buildings that told these stories. It was the hills, and the cold inhumanity, the luster and boredom of the sea.

2. THE OLD PHILOSOPHERS

Theorists who hold life and art completely separate are killing the thing they supposedly love. The word "text" as it is used by many critics now fills me with anger, because it so often reduces history or literature to a system of arbitrary codes, interpretations rather than events. By contrast, even a philosophical poet like Wallace Stevens was clearly concerned with being in the world, noticing oranges and coffee as much as the poem about oranges and coffee. Yes, the poem about the orange is not the orange, but it influences our awareness of the orange. The sermon about death is not death, but the dead body is a fact beyond interpretation. In Plato's *Phaedo*, Socrates waxes wise about the life after death, adding that "no reasonable man ought to insist that the facts are exactly as I have described them." Then he drinks the hemlock and dies slowly from the feet up. We are left with the body, but also with a question: What happened? We may be aware that accounts of the death are open to interpretation, just as the dialogues of Plato subvert their own assertions by offering more than one voice. But the body is a fact beyond interpretation. History may be composed of texts, but it is also composed of dead and living bodies. Our interpretation of events is not the events themselves, and truth matters even when we doubt our ability to know it.

For Stevens, who successfully navigated the world of business yet enjoyed meditative walks or quiet moments alone in a New York cathedral, human existence was a symbiosis of the real and the imagined. In his beautiful lecture, "The Noble Rider and the Sound of Words," delivered at Princeton in wartime, he speaks of "the pressure of reality," by which he particularly means the sort of catastrophic global events anyone could read about in the daily papers. The pressure was indeed great, as German, Italian and Japanese nationalists advanced on all fronts. Stevens felt that, in our society, the imagination was also losing ground to this "pressure of reality." The world of facts which he inhabited every day had little use for an imagined nobility.

Nobility, Stevens said, was a force, and imaginative activities like poetry were needed to keep it alive in the world:

It is not an artifice that the mind has added to human nature. The mind has added nothing to human nature. It is a violence from within that protects us from the violence without. It is the imagination pressing back against the pressure of reality. It seems, in the last analysis, to have something to do with our self-preservation; and that, no doubt, is why the expression of it, the sound of its words, helps us live our lives.

This most reticent and philosophical of poets actually declared that poetry helps us live our lives! It is more than a closed system of interpretations. It speaks to us and in us. Sometimes it even ennobles us. It is a way of being in the world.

Of course, poetry is only one of the arts and only one kind of imaginative organization. But these activities have indeed been helpful, preserving some part of us even as we preserve them. The classical scholar Bernard Knox recalls a moment in World War II when poetry and life intersected for him. A member of the OSS who saw plenty of action, he found himself in 1944 fighting the Germans alongside Italian partisans in the mountains south of Modena. At one point, huddled in a ruined house under fire from a German machine gun, he picked up a copy of Virgil in the debris, "one of a series of classical texts issued by the Royal Italian Academy to celebrate the greatness of ancient (and modern) Rome; the title page bore the improbable heading, in Latin, IUSSU BENEDICTI MUSSOLINI — 'By Order of Benito Mussolini.' " Knox tells this story in the introduction to his *Essays Ancient & Modern* by way of explaining his subsequent career as a scholar. Recalling that Virgil's poems had once been thought prophetic, he opened the book to a passage from the first Georgic, which he translates as follows:

> Here right and wrong are reversed; so many wars in the world, so many faces of evil. The plow is despised and rejected; the farmers marched off, the field untended. The curving sickles are beaten straight to make swords. On one side the East moves to war on the other, Germany. Neighboring cities tear up their treaties and take to arms; the vicious war god rages the world over.

Knox's meditation on these words and the moment of finding them strikes me as a beautiful example of the poetry of life and the life of poetry:

> These lines, written thirty years before the birth of Christ, expressed, more directly and passionately than any modern statement I know of, the reality of the world I was living in: the shell-pocked, mine-infested fields, the shattered cities and the starving population of that Italy Virgil so loved, the misery of the whole world at war. And there was in fact a sort of prophecy in it. "On one side the East moves to war." I did not know it yet, but the unit in which I served was to be selected for a role in the main Japanese landing, which was already in the planning stage. In this case, luckily for all of us, the Virgilian oracle was wrong.

> It was time to move up. I tried to get the book into one of my pockets, but it was too big and I threw it down. But as we ran and crawled through the rubble I thought to myself: "If I ever get out of this, I'm going back to the classics and study them seriously."

This full-time avocation, literature, has much to do with life as we live it, searching for our place in the narrative of humankind.

It may be that I am telling too many war stories here—especially for someone who, thankfully, has no experience of warfare. But these tales of extremity only confirm what I also feel about so-called ordinary life: that the world we imagine and the world we inhabit with our bodies are deeply related.

Now I recall the case of Patrick Leigh Fermor, the great English writer who lives in southern Greece. For a time I was his neighbor, my one-room hut sharing an edenic bay with his more spacious villa. I remember lying in my hammock on a summer night while Fermor's opera recordings drifted to me over the olives and cypresses. The breeze off the mountains cooled me; the grating cicadas quit their racket when the sun went down. I had no electricity in that little house, so I read his books by lamplight, devouring everything he had written to impress him with my knowledge of it when we met. His prose was so rich that it made me hungry, and I actually had to eat bread and cheese while reading. His words increased my appetite for language and experience.

I was twenty-five years old; to me Leigh Fermor represented a literary ideal, the intellectual and physical life melded in one Byronic personality. Years later, while I plodded through graduate school, I frequently envied his alternative to a college education — in the early 1930s he had walked from the Hook of Holland to Constantinople (even the use of that name is fraught with historical significance). He was also legendary for his involvement with the Cretan resistance during World War II, having masterminded their kidnapping of Major-General Heinrich Kreipe, the commander of the German garrison. Leigh Fermor has never told the full story of these events, choosing instead to translate a Greek version by George Psychoundakis. But in *A Time of Gifts*, the first volume of his masterful travel-memoir, Leigh Fermor relates a story not unlike that of Bernard Knox:

> The hazards of war landed me among the crags of occupied Crete with a band of Cretan guerrillas and a captive German general whom we had waylaid and carried off into the mountains three days before. The German garrison of the island were in hot, but luckily temporarily misdirected, chase. It was a time of anxiety and danger; and for our captive, of hardship and distress. During a lull in the pursuit, we woke up among the rocks just as a brilliant dawn was breaking over the crest of Mount Ida. We had been toiling over it, through snow and then rain, for the last two days. Looking across the valley at this flashing mountain-crest, the general murmured to himself:
>
> > Vides ut alta stet nive candidum
> > Soracte...
>
> It was one of the ones I knew! I continued from where he had left off:
>
> > nec iam sustineant onus
> > Silvae laborantes, geluque
> > Flumina constiterint acuto,
>
> and so on, through the remaining five stanzas to the end. The general's blue eyes swiveled away from the mountain-top to mine—

and when I'd finished, after a long silence, he said: "Ach so, Herr Major!" It was very strange. As though, for a long moment, the war had ceased to exist. We had both drunk at the same fountain long before; and things were different between us for the rest of our time together.

I remember arguing with a friend about this scene.[1] The friend thought it preposterous, declaring that a Hollywood cliché of noble aristocracy had found its way into Leigh Fermor's memory, and then into his book. But I had ample opportunity to observe his recall of verse in several languages. It was another aspect of his character I had admired and tried to imitate. I also knew that, despite the objections of cynics, people do remember poems or songs or key phrases at surprising moments in life, as if pressing back against the pressure of reality.

Another soldier, Field-Marshal A.P. Wavell, demonstrated his prodigious memory for verse by collecting a 400-page anthology from memory. *Other Men's Flowers*, published in 1944, comprised only poems that Wavell had by heart. He acknowledged that his choices would seem old fashioned to some, but the anthology does have its treasures, like the Kipling I quote at the beginning of this essay. My point about Wavell is that he was a practical man, a soldier whose 1916 wound cost him the sight in one eye, a masterful strategist whose 1941 book, *Generals and Generalship*, was read and re-read by Erwin Rommel, and finally, he was one of the last Viceroys of India. Yet this man needed poetry and knew that others needed it. *Other Men's Flowers* sold extremely well, and in his Preface to the revised edition Wavell paid homage to one of his readers:

> A tribute which I greatly valued came in the form of an annotated copy which a friend sent me. The annotations had been made by a soldier who read *Other Men's Flowers* during the period of his final training for D-Day in Normandy. As he read each poem he put the date on which and sometimes the circumstances in which he had read it; and added his comments of enjoyment, indifference or dislike. He had finished the volume while crossing to Normandy and had fallen in the battle shortly afterwards. I often turn up that copy

and read the comments, which reveal a fine, somewhat puritan, character and shrewd judgment. I am proud that my selection should have helped him in those days, and that it was on the whole to his taste. I hope I may have helped and entertained many such others.

This poetry was not intended to be patriotic propaganda gearing the soldier's mind for war; it was intended to help and entertain. Though Wavell's choices would surely not meet the approval of most academic critics now, I find his anthology strangely moving because it was made by a man who believed in poetry's sustaining power. He knew that the best forms of expression are often those we want most to remember.

Life appears on occasion to have form, to borrow its form from poetry even as poetry borrows from life. I return to Wallace Stevens, this time his wartime poem, "Notes Toward a Supreme Fiction":

> Soldier, there is a war between the mind
> And Sky, between thought and day and night. It is
> For that the poet is always in the sun,
>
> Patches the moon together in his room
> To his Virgilian cadences, up down,
> Up down. It is a war that never ends.
>
> Yet it depends on yours. The two are one.
> They are a plural, a right and left, a pair,
> Two parallels that meet if only in
>
> The meeting of their shadows or that meet
> In a book in a barrack, a letter from Malay.

Poetry needn't always refer to the world in a straightforward manner, just as the world is frequently not straightforward with us. The spell of nonsense is as important as the elegy or prayer. We can hope poetry that matters is remembered, brought into our lives out of need or pleasure. The pleasure in a line may not be universal, the need may be weaker than our need for water, but poetry has proven tenacious in its survival.

When I read poetry in college I was taught to be impersonal, always impersonal, as if to avoid contaminating what I read. Now it seems to me that the force of personality is every bit as important as the mastery of craft. Reading and writing are an invitation to a great untidy conversation that spans generations and cultures. The idea that we must be impersonal derives partly from T.S. Eliot, but did anyone ever really believe that Eliot was not present in his poems? That wan smile, the self so distanced from itself, that nearly Buddhist monasticism and sly humor are all there. We have the *Waste Land* manuscript with Vivienne Eliot's "WONDERFUL" scrawled next to what seems a weirdly confessional passage. And we have the two volumes of Lyndall Gordon's critical biography, the fullest discussion yet of the interplay of life and art in Eliot's career.

Eliot's early denial of personality, especially in "Tradition and the Individual Talent," was rooted in his own psychological defenses, as well as in his talent for philosophical and religious abstraction. But this denial rapidly became doctrine, easily misinterpreted by droves of readers and writers. Eliot himself constantly revised his position on the matter, and his later work—especially *Four Quartets* and *The Family Reunion*—is decidedly confessional.

"Discoveries in art...," wrote Marianne Moore, "are personal before they are general." There must be various levels of detachment in both life and art. The detachment of artists from their craft is a simple necessity, and Modernists were obsessed with craft, with remaking the forms of expression. When Eliot separates "the man who suffers and the mind which creates" he may well be neurotic, but it is the defining neurosis of art. His desire to direct criticism to the poem and not the poet is also extremely helpful, leading to the technique of "close reading" in the classroom and in most academic criticism. Nowadays close reading often bores me; I long to attach discussions of poetry to discussions of everything else. But close, even impersonal reading remains an essential skill for students to master, and we should acknowledge the useful legacy of Eliot's ideas.

Once at a literary gathering a poet asked me whom I enjoyed reading—this was in about 1982. I harkened back to the early poems of Eliot, some of which I had memorized while in high school.

When I mentioned this, the poet turned on one heel and marched away from me in righteous indignation. To admire Eliot was, in certain circles, tantamount to admiring an impersonal royalist snob. Worse, it was like admiring the desiccated corpse of the Western tradition. I can only say that most dismissals of Eliot appear to have been made by people who have not read the full range of his criticism. His arguments against a wholly secular society, for example, now seem prescient in some ways. He saw that the materialism of a consumer culture was insufficient to ensure our survival; in *The Idea of a Christian Society* his environmental position is nearly indistinguishable from that of the Sierra Club.

Eliot also modified his ideas about impersonality, especially in his 1940 essay on Yeats, where he explored "two forms of impersonality: that which is natural to the skilled craftsman, and that which is more and more achieved by the maturing artist." Yeats, he said, began as the former but became the latter. In other words, it is possible for a poet to be passionately local yet convey "a general truth." Universality is suspect in some quarters, I suppose, but I would submit that we cannot have great art without it. For better or worse, Eliot influenced writers all over the world: Montale, Seferis and Achebe come immediately to mind. Dante, Shakespeare and Yeats have had similarly global influence, which suggests that the particularities of their art have not impeded their expressions of general truths. The argument against masterpieces of this magnitude is an argument for an exclusively local poetry, which would be severely limiting. Wallace Stevens' friend, George Santayana, wrote that "The sole advantage in possessing great works of literature lies in what they can help us to become." Perhaps this was what led Stevens to declare that poetry helps us live our lives. I do not think either man meant this simplistically. Poetry is not quite bread; it does not feed the refugees who feel the pressure of reality so intensely now. But it is an awareness, a verbal precision that offers flashes of lucidity.

One of the greatest modern commentators on the poetry of life and the life of poetry was W.H. Auden. Everyone remembers his declaration that "poetry makes nothing happen," but few recall his modification of it, his insistence on poetry's survival as "A way of happening, a mouth." No modern poet was more acutely aware of the distance between political or religious experiences and their expression in poetry. As he said in *New Year Letter*:

> Art in intention is mimesis
> But, realized, the resemblance ceases;
> Art is not life, and cannot be
> A midwife to society,
> For art is a *fait accompli*....

Like Robert Frost, Auden called poetry a game and denied its practicality. But both poets understood its usefulness for our consciousness of being in the world. Like his literary godfather, Eliot, Auden spoke of impersonality in poetry, wrongly suggesting that his biography would reveal nothing of importance about his art. But *The Dyer's Hand* makes it clear that Auden did not believe absolutely in the separation of life and art:

> Speaking for myself, the questions which interest me most when reading a poem are two. The first is technical: "Here is a verbal contraption. How does it work?" The second is, in the broadest sense, moral: "What kind of a guy inhabits this poem? What is his notion of the good life or the good place? His notion of the Evil One? What does he conceal from the reader? What does he conceal even from himself?"

Auden believed that the social nature of language precluded any absolutely private or solipsistic writing. "There are other social animals who have signal codes," he wrote, "...but only man has a language by means of which he can disclose himself to his neighbor, which he could not do and would not want to do if he did not first possess the capacity and need to disclose himself to himself."

We may feel isolated from each other, from God, from any meaning we have desired, but the language of poetry can't help being a kind of ceremony. It insists, sometimes against all reason, that we are not alone, that our most intimate or noble, trivial or terrible natures are already understood.

For a poet one possible ambition is to write something so beautiful, so precise, so true, that another person, preferably many people, would choose to remember it. We may never agree on some ultimate canon of literature, but the belief in masterpieces, in great books, is essential to cultural survival.

When I was in college I read Yeats. I did not understand him, even when I had read Richard Ellmann's clarifications of his life and work, but I was besotted by the poetry. After college I refused to read Yeats for six years, fearing that his personality would completely overwhelm my own.

Language entered me through the ear; my mind lagged far behind in its development. When I was sixteen I read the Benjy section of William Faulkner's *The Sound and the Fury* while driving a pea combine in the Skagit Valley. The combines were gigantic shucking cylinders hauled behind diesel tractors. We drove slowly in the summer heat, the dust and chaff flying thick about us. In a forty-acre field I could get a page or two read while inching down a single row of swathed pea vines. I did not understand a word I was reading, but the poetry of Faulkner's voice entered and became part of my life. Benjy's sad vulnerability and hyper-awareness of the natural world got under my skin. Later, Eugene O'Neill's wretched family became mine, though it turns out that I was far luckier than O'Neill. Eliot's "Preludes" made perfect sense, but only as mood, as tone—I had never seen gaslights or cab horses, and knew nothing of his philosophy. I was moved by his vision of vulnerable people, and my teenage cynicism found confirmation in the poem's abrupt closure: "The worlds revolve like ancient women / Gathering fuel in vacant lots."

In college I extolled difficult literature that I did not understand. I remember sitting at the family dinner table one vacation when my older brother insisted that I explain why Faulkner was a great writer. I could not, because I did not understand what my ear had taken in. My brother mocked me, and I left the table in tears.

Something else happened to me on one of those vacations. I attempted to write the following anecdote into a short story, which I showed to my favorite professor; he told me that the story was full of inaccuracies. People just didn't behave the way I had them behave. "People don't walk around quoting poetry," he said. About most of the story he was surely right, but not that last remark. People do quote poetry, or refer to it—some do, anyway—and they connect it to their lives.

My parents had been divorced for years when this happened. I won't go into the gory details, except to say that in hindsight their divorce has the inevitability of art. It too was set in motion by the war, or events long before the war. My mother had raised my brothers and me through hard times. Both of my parents endured hard times, but I am particularly concerned here with my mother. She was dating a man who had taught me to play chess years before, and who took an active interest in my love of reading. On one of my trips home from college I had brought my selected Yeats, and after dinner I sat in the living room with this man and my mother, talking about the Irish poet.

My mother was a psychology professor, and, though our house was full of books, I had never thought of her as someone who read poetry. She surprised me by saying there was a poem of Yeats she especially liked, and asked to borrow my book. While she leafed through it, looking for the poem, I tried to show off my knowledge to her indulgent friend.

At last she found the poem. She did not read it aloud, but passed the book to me so I could see what she had indicated. Here is the poem I read silently that night:

> Others because you did not keep
> That deep-sworn vow have been friends of mine;
> Yet always when I look death in the face,
> When I clamber to the heights of sleep,
> Or when I grow excited with wine,
> Suddenly I meet your face.

Of course I did not understand it at the time. She was talking to me through Yeats, using the poem to explain her life to me. She wanted me to know that she still loved my father, despite all the hell they put each other through. Yeats's voice speaks across time. It is specific to his life, his loves and prejudices. Yet it becomes one of our voices too, the imagination pressing back against the pressure of reality. The poetry of life and the life of poetry mean that reality alone is no place to live.

[1] Leigh Fermor quotes Horace's Odes (I. ix). Here is John Dryden's 1685 version of the stanza:

> Behold yon mountain's hoary height,
>   Made higher with new mounts of snow;
> Again, behold the winter weight
>   Oppress the laboring woods below;
> And streams with icy fetters bound
> Benumbed and cramped to solid ground

Homage to W. H. Auden

MILES FROM BABYLON:
POEMS OF THE UNFINISHED JOURNEY

The self is difficult to apprehend outside a specific location, yet so many of us are frequently restless. Thinking about one place suggests other places. We tell stories of real life, our purgatorial happiness, our formal despair, and stories suggest a future or past wholeness, as in this nursery rhyme:

> How many miles to Babylon?
> Three score miles and ten.
> Can I get there by candlelight?
> Yes, and back again.
> If your heels are nimble and light,
> You can get there by candlelight.

What is Babylon? A lullaby's babyland? A dream? A promised land? Our mythologies of elsewhere are endless: Eden, the New Jerusalem, Mecca, California, Atlantis, Ithaca, Byzantium, the Good Place, the Just City. It is the place where we are not—beyond us, yet imagined by us. The Biblical three score and ten is reimagined as a journey in spatial terms. As Pascal wrote (in the translation of A.J. Krailsheimer), "All our life passes in this way: we seek rest by struggling against certain obstacles, and once they are overcome, rest proves intolerable because of the boredom it produces. We must get away from it and crave excitement." Travel is travail. Motion is a philosophical position, an entertainment of possibilities.

Poetry, too, is a kind of motion, often a verbal pacing. When you travel, you are like Theseus in his maze, following the string that connects you to some desired goal—except, of course, the string is invisible or imagined. We perceive a connection, a continuity that we attempt to enact with our bodies. Travel is estrangement, a glancing awareness of where we are and where we are not. Poetry is also an attempt to embody connection, literally to give voice to some essential bond that was long ago broken, perhaps in infancy, or in the very sources of human consciousness. I would like to look briefly at three poems—by Yeats, Auden, and Cavafy—in which motion is the whole point. In many ways these are poems of non-arrival, poems in which the lullaby promises nothing more than itself, the voice babbling on about Babylon, or perhaps there is a candlelit nimbleness, a nod and a wink. But there is no real arrival, no point at which actual and imagined destinations coincide.

Well, you may ask is any poet a poet of arrival? I'm not sure. In "Sailing to Byzantium," Yeats rages at a world in which life is "begotten, born and dies." The poem is almost too perfect in it avowal of art's permanence : "And therefore I have sailed the seas and come/ To the holy city of Byzantium." I have arrived, he says, and the great vehicle of arrival is art. Yeats's poetry contains a dualism of body and soul, politics and the imagination. His lofty disdain for the common man implies that the artist is a superior form of traveler; the artist reaches a Byzantium that is inaccessible to the rest of us. But "Sailing to Byzantium" is not quite so lofty as I make it sound. Yeats is a poet of motion more than of stasis. He asks for permanence in lines that are full of the violent awareness of human frailty. If he is closer to Byzantium than you or I, he is, nevertheless, like us, mortal:

> O sages standing in God's holy fire
> As in the gold mosaic of a wall,
> Come from the holy fire, perne in a gyre,
> And be the singing-masters of my soul.
> Consume my heart away; sick with desire
> And fastened to a dying animal
> It knows not what it is; and gather me
> Into the artifice of eternity.

Yeats's arrival is qualified, as I suppose it must be. His poem is dynamic, though one could argue that the perfections of its final stanza, its resolute and ramifying closure, defy all modesty. Yeats owes his power and the lyric tension of his lines to the tug of this defiance against the downward pull of gravity.

Perhaps Yeats differs from Auden most in his notion of just who the traveller is. In Yeats it is "old men," but I think we could also find plenty of evidence in his work that it is really the poet. Poetry may begin in the "foul rag and bone shop of the heart," as he says in another famous poem, but the poet has a distinct edge over that "raving slut who keeps the till." In Auden the travelers are you and

I. Auden's poetry often displays a dualistic tension like Yeats's, but he rarely seems a poet for an ivory tower. "The notion of the alienated artist," he wrote in a review of Thomas Mann's *Tonio Kröger,* is a phenomenon of the second half of the nineteenth century. In earlier times we do not find it and, in our own, alienation has become almost a universal problem." How are we alienated? Let me count the ways. Better still, let Pascal tell us:

> We perceive an image of the truth and possess nothing but falsehood, being equally incapable of absolute ignorance and certain knowledge; so obvious is it that we once enjoyed a degree of perfection from which we have unhappily fallen.

Like Pascal, Auden saw the human condition as a fallen one. Eden is a metaphor for lost wholeness, babyland, Babylon—miles and miles away.

When he wrote "Atlantis" in January 1941, Auden had been in America exactly two years, and Yeats had been dead for the same amount of time. The power of Yeats as an example for Auden is indisputable, and it is clear that Auden struggled to work free of the older poet's bardic influence. His work on the long didactic poem *New Year Letter* and the operetta *Paul Bunyan,* his experiments with prose and syllabics, neoclassicism and the music hall, demonstrate his energetic searches for a technical range and territory he could call his own. Auden was always an original, but the death of Yeats in 1939 surely left him with some anxiety of influence, which he promptly exorcised in his poetry.

Because "Atlantis" is seldom anthologized and will be unfamiliar to many readers, I quote the entire poem here:

> Being set on the idea
> > Of getting to Atlantis,
> You will have discovered of course
> > Only the Ship of Fools is
> Making the voyage this year,
> As gales of abnormal force
> > Are predicted, and that you
> > Must therefore be ready to

Behave absurdly enough
        To pass for one of the Boys,
At least appearing to love
        Hard liquor, horseplay and noise.

Should storms, as may well happen,
        Drive you to anchor a week
In some old harbour-city
        Of Ionia, then speak
With her witty scholars, men
Who have proved there cannot be
        Such a place as Atlantis:
        Learn their logic, but notice
How its subtlety betrays
        Their simple enormous grief;
Thus they shall teach you the ways
        To doubt that you may believe.

If, later, you run aground
        Among the headlands of Thrace,
Where with torches all night long
        A naked barbaric race
Leaps frenziedly to the sound
Of conch and dissonant gong;
        On that savage stoney shore
        Strip off your clothes and dance, for
Unless you are capable
        Of forgetting completely
About Atlantis, you will
        Never finish your journey.

Again, should you come to gay
        Carthage or Corinth, take part
In their endless gaiety;
        And if in some bar a tart,
As she strokes your hair, should say
"This is Atlantis, dearie,"
        Listen with attentiveness
        To her life-story. Unless

You become acquainted now
    With each refuge that tries to
Counterfeit Atlantis, how
    Will you recognize the true?

Assuming you beach at last
    Near Atlantis, and begin
The terrible trek inland
    Through squalid woods and frozen
Tundras where all are soon lost;
If forsaken then, you stand,
    Dismissal everywhere,
    Stone and snow, silence and air,
O remember the great dead
    And honour the fate you are,
Traveling and tormented,
    Dialectic and bizarre.

Stagger onward rejoicing;
    And even then if, perhaps
Having actually got
    To the last col, you collapse
With all Atlantis shining
Below you yet you cannot
    Descend, you should still be proud
    Even to have been allowed
Just to peep at Atlantis
    In a poetic vision:
Give thanks and lie down in peace,
    Having seen your salvation.

All the little household gods
    Have started crying, but say
Good-bye now, and put to sea.
    Farewell, my dear, farewell: may
Hermes, master of the roads,
And the four dwarf Kabiri
    Protect and serve you always;
    And may the Ancient of Days

> Provide for all you must do
> His invisible guidance,
> Lifting up, dear, upon you
> The light of His countenance.

On one level, "Atlantis" can be read as a comic revision of "Sailing to Byzantium." The first thing I notice is the urbane opening sentence with its subversion of conventional technique. It's not just that he writes in heptasyllabic lines, but also that he breaks the lines without any concern for lyric tension. Look at line 7: "Are predicted, and that you..."; it doesn't contain a single important word! There is no lyrical magic here, and all assertions are made in a spirit of civilized play. Auden refers to the traveler in the second person which, despite evidence that he had a specific person in mind, effectively points to the reader. You—I—we are going on this journey. The poet has no more importance than the rest of us. I also notice the comedy of his rhymes, particularly "idea" and "year," "Boys" and "noise." Auden depletes the occasion of importance because this quest is not exceptional; it is universal. We are "set on the idea/ Of getting to Atlantis...." We are not there, and we will never, in fact, arrive. The Ship of Fools would include us, and it looks as though we will enjoy ourselves despite "gales of abnormal force" (this was a wartime poem).

It is possible that we could be satisfied with one of these partial explanations—the lie of the tart "As she strokes your hair," for example. But assuming that you go on—again I draw your attention to Auden's wry ambivalence—"Assuming you beach at last/ Near Atlantis," what exactly is promised you? Nothing but a "terrible trek inland," which may be much like a visit to Yeats's "foul rag and bone shop." Auden sends up all the heroic archetypes of exploration and art: the frozen tundras and lost shipmates, the hero dismissed by a cold universe. The line "Stagger onward rejoicing" expresses Auden's stance toward life and art as well as any that he wrote, but look what he follows it with: "And even then if, perhaps...." The very idea of poetic resonance, of the line itself, is shot down without apparent regret. The poetic vision is not the poet's exclusive province. We are all "Traveling and tormented/ Dialectic and bizarre." And it is possible to be grateful for this, grateful for the surprise of rhyme and the slightest apprehension of some ultimate arrival. It's a bit like standing naked in a blizzard and being happy that you have a cup of coffee around which to warm your hands.

Auden ends "Atlantis" as he ended *New Year Letter*, with a prayer. Perhaps the best a poet can do is to sketch what the journey might be like and offer a benediction. He calls on Hermes, who was a patron of travelers. He calls upon the Kabiri, deities of Phrygian origin responsible for both fertility and the preservation of mariners. He includes the God named in the Book of Daniel, but the operative word in Auden's blessing, "may," is calculated to disabuse the traveler of any certainties. If each of its stanzas is an allegory of a kind of travel or exploration, perhaps prayer is our ultimate recourse or refuge—the ultimate function of language and poetry , yet suggestive of the ultimate estrangement.

In 1961 Auden wrote an introduction to *The Complete Poems of Cavafy* (translated by Rae Dalven) which begins as follows:

> Ever since I was first introduced to his poetry by the late
> Professor R. M. Dawkins over thirty years ago, C. P.
> Cavafy has remained an influence on my own writing;
> that is to say, I can think of poems which, if Cavafy
> were unknown to me, I should have written quite
> differently or perhaps not written at all.

Whether "Atlantis" was one of the poems Auden had in mind I cannot say, but it bears striking resemblance to Cavafy's "Ithaca." *Pharos and Pharillon*, a 1923 book by E. M. Forster (who would later befriend Auden), had done much to introduce Cavafy's work to the English-speaking world. In 1924 T. S. Eliot's *Criterion* published a translation of "Ithaca" by George Valassopoulos—perhaps later Auden ran across it when looking through back numbers of the magazine that would publish his own early poems. There have been numerous subsequent translations, of course, and Auden's Oxford contemporary, Rex Wamer, eventually wrote an introduction to translations by John Mavrogordato.

"Ithaca" may have attracted English readers because of its faint echoes of Tennyson's "Ulysses," but it also plays with ideas of incompletion, the nature of journeys and the inconclusiveness of their conclusions, themes which attracted such modernists as Pound and Eliot. Here is Rae Dalven's version of the poem:

When you start on your journey to Ithaca,
then pray that the road is long,
full of adventure, full of knowledge.
Do not fear the Lestrygonians
and the Cyclopes and the angry Poseidon.
You will never meet such as these on your path,
if your thoughts remain lofty, if a fine
emotion touches your body and your spirit.
You will never meet the Lestrygonians,
the Cyclopes and the fierce Poseidon,
if you do not carry them within your soul,
if your soul does not raise them up before you.

Then pray that the road is long.
That the summer mornings are many,
that you will enter ports seen for the first time
with such pleasure, with such joy!
Stop at Phoenician markets,
and purchase fine merchandise,
mother-of-pearl and corals, amber and ebony,
and pleasurable perfumes of all kinds,
buy as many pleasurable perfumes as you can;
visit hosts of Egyptian cities,
to learn and learn from those who have knowledge.

Always keep Ithaca fixed in your mind.
To arrive there is your ultimate goal.
But do not hurry the voyage at all.
It is better to let it last for long years;
and even to anchor at the isle when you are old,
rich with all that you have gained on the way,
not expecting that Ithaca will offer you riches.

Ithaca has given you the beautiful voyage.
Without her you would never have taken the road.
But she has nothing more to give you.
And if you find her poor, Ithaca has not defrauded you.
With the great wisdom you have gained, with so much experience,
you must surely have understood by then what Ithacas mean.

Like "Sailing to Byzantium" and "Atlantis," "Ithaca" names a port and, more significantly, names a desire for arrival. Similarities to "Atlantis" are particularly striking. Both Cavafy and Auden stress enjoyment of the journey, with none of Yeats's frustration with physical imperfection. Both Cavafy and Auden use prayer at the hopeful beginning of their journeys. They suggest that we cannot begin with expectations, only with hopes and an open spirit.

The key difference among the three poets is in their choice of myths. Yeats's Byzantium is less an historical civilization than a kind of formal perfection — "out of nature" in more ways than one. Auden chooses the city of Plato's parable, something lost or hidden from view or, more ominous, about to sink under the ocean. Cavafy's destination is home. We've already been there. Like Odysseus, we began in our Ithaca, knew it intimately, and have carried its image, its textures and aromas throughout the world. For Cavafy the path moves back to some ancestral intimacy. Yet without Ithaca "you would never have taken the road." This is the paradoxical heart of the matter. We begin with wholeness. The trauma of broken bonds sends us traveling in search of reunion — at least that is the usual version of the story. Cavafy's poem is closer to Pascal: we chose to leave our Ithaca because we could not bear her and we desired the painful wisdom of separation as much as we desired the pleasure of return. We are "traveling and tormented," Auden says, but Cavafy tells us to "Pray that the road is long." Both poems arise from the same intuition of incompleteness, the same curiosity about what the grass looks like on the other side of the fence. Both invite us — all of us, not just the poets — to look for ourselves.

I think the anxiety underlying these poems (and it is anxiety, despite their good humor) is basic, perhaps even universal. It begins when we come crying into this world, deepens as we learn how broad a gulf there is in every word we speak. Words themselves are artifacts of estrangement; languages grow in the ruins of the tower of Babel, and poems are vessels sent out to trade in distant lands. I suppose it is possible that in some human cultures this anxiety does not exist, but I have never known those cultures, nor do I think that self-imposed exiles like Auden and Cavafy knew them. Perhaps we make it to Babylon only in the candlelight of the nursery rhyme. The older I am, the more uncertain I become of my destination, though I may very well pray that the road is long.

AUDEN ONSTAGE

> You alone, alone, imaginary song,
> Are unable to say an existence is wrong,
> And pour out your forgiveness like a wine.
>
> —"The Composer"

Auden's poetry delights in wisdom, finds wisdom in delight. He was one of the greatest lyric poets of our language, yet he worked in forms "large enough to swim in" for his entire career. In musical dramas, radio plays, film scripts, an oratorio, long didactic poems, opera libretti and verse sequences, his philosophical mind pushed him tirelessly beyond his lyric gift, as if the forgiveness of song were not entirely to he trusted. In 1937, Christopher Isherwood wrote of his friend and collaborator, "If Auden had his way, he would turn every play into a cross between grand opera and high mass." Now that Auden's plays and libretti are gathered in the first two volumes of his *Complete Works,* it becomes apparent that he got his way. He pioneered a new allegorical drama, and made the most significant contribution to opera libretti since Hugo von Hofmannsthal. Like the tumbler in his "Ballad of Barnaby," Auden discovered a sacred joy in the varied practice of his craft. When readers realize that these two hefty volumes don't even contain Auden's major work (the poems and prose are yet to come), they may well be awestruck at his monumental energy.

Not everything assembled here is monumental, however, or even good. Slogging through bits of *The Fronny,* all of *The Enemies of a Bishop and The Chase* (early versions of Auden and Isherwood's uneven play *The Dog Beneath the Skin),* I wondered who was served by this attempt to publish a great poet's every doodle. Would Auden have approved? But despite my reservations about these big compendia that cost a kingpin's ransom, I think Auden would have admired the loyal scholarship of Edward Mendelson. It was Auden, after all, who found Yeats's disparaging poem, "The Scholars," libelous: "Edit indeed; Thank God they do. If it had not been for scholars working themselves blind copying and collating manuscripts, how many poems would be unavailable...?" Poets are best represented by their best work, but the Auden canon has always been problematic because of his obsessive revisions and the sheer bulk of his production in so many different genres. The only solution is to scrape every iota of Auden together, set it in some reasonable order and let the reader decide. Mendelson is just the scholar for the job, an excellent textual editor, and both of these volumes do contain treasures rescued from oblivion.

Those willing to read the lesser works collected here, along with the masterpieces and Mendelson's rich notes in the back of each volume, will find fascinating evidence of Auden's prodigious mind. Like the medieval craftsmen he admired, he approached each new literary task as an apprenticeship. We can see Auden and Isherwood learning about dramatic structure here, and how Auden the librettist (together with Chester Kallman) taught himself not only to write verses that could be set to music, but to rethink the dramatic structure of opera.

Auden's first play was a solo effort, *Paid on Both Sides* (1928), a charade intended for performance at the home of an Oxford friend. It bears several earmarks of Auden's theatrical work: a mixture of prose and verse, the latter often with an alliterative Anglo-Saxon cast, and an avoidance of realism in character and scene. Even with some schoolboy silliness, its story of a bloody feud between the Nowers and the Shaws has a haunting power. Like much early Auden, the play deals with borders and the banal violence of families or nations, a world where the secret self figures as a doomed spy. Mendelson has given us two versions of the script, allowing us to see how Auden revised and deepened it. In the second version, John Nower experiences a dream vision of the mysterious Man-Woman, "a prisoner of war behind barbed wire, in the snow." This androgynous figure berates Nower for his superficial life: "Love was not love for you but episodes, /Traffic in memoirs, views from different sides...." The hero emerges from his dream changed as though by psychotherapy, able to turn away from boyish alliances and love Anne Shaw, the daughter of his enemy. John and Anne are the doomed lovers who will recur in Auden's works for the stage, especially *On the Frontier, The Rake's Progress* and *Elegy for Young Lovers* (versions of this impossible love are also found in his poems, "Lullaby," "As I Walked Out One Evening" and *The Age of Anxiety*). Love is a momentary, perhaps delusional return to the wholeness of Eden. It is intoxicating and dangerous, and Auden's lovers usually know that it cannot last:

> But loving now let none
> Think of divided days
> When we shall choose from ways,
> All of them evil, one.

Anne Shaw's family executes her lover, unwittingly preserving the violent doubleness of a fallen world.

"Damn realism," Auden wrote in his 1929 journal. "Yet it must be real." And in a later entry: "A Play is poetry of action." At about the same time, Auden and Isherwood composed their "Preliminary Statement" or embryonic manifesto on the theatre. Here one can find Audenesque pronouncements on the psychosomatic nature of illness and its correlation to the ills of society, but also statements like "Dramatic action is ritual" and "Dramatic plot is the assertion that God could not exist without Satan." Auden thought of theatre in allegorical terms, and thought poetry as ritual more important than prosaic realism. In a 1938 lecture he would state that "the search for a dramatic form is very closely bound up with something much wider and more important, which is the search for a society which is both free and unified." Despite the experimental quality of his plays, Auden clearly loved theatre's social aspect; he was a natural collaborator.

We should also remember that Auden wrote musicals. Lyrics for *The Dance of Death* and *The Dog Beneath the Skin* (a.k.a. *Dogskin*) were given a score by Herbert Murrill, and the best of them found their way into Auden's collections of verse. His eerily premonitory "Witnesses," for example, first appeared in *The Chase:*

> Climb up the crane, learn the sailor's words
> When the ships from the islands laden with birds
>   Come in
> Tell your stories of fishing and other men's wives
> The expansive moments of constricted lives
>   In the lighted inn.

But do not imagine we do not know
Nor that what you hide with such care won't show
    At a glance.
Nothing is done, nothing is said
But don't make the mistake of believing us dead
    I shouldn't dance.

We're afraid in that case you'll have a fall
We've been watching you over the garden wall
    For hours
The sky is darkening like a stain
Something is going to fall like rain
    An it won't be flowers.

Even the dialogue in these poetic dramas sometimes reads like a trio or duet, as though Auden were already the librettist-in-training.

Isherwood thought of Auden as the musical half of their team; in a 1965 interview with George Wickes he said,

> The whole collaboration really amounted to this: here was Auden, who was obviously already a major poet, and all I felt I was doing was perhaps providing a slightly firmer framework on which these poems could be presented. I don't mean that Auden was incapable of dramaturgy because as a matter of fact he did a great many of the scenes. But my real function was very much that of a librettist, and he was the composer.

Auden had similarly modest things to say about his own contributions to both the plays and the libretti. The point is that it took him and Isherwood some time to get beyond a sort of musical review — stringing lyrics on a convoluted and amateurish plot — to plays with tight dramatic structures. They succeeded only twice, in *The Ascent of F6* and *On the Frontier*. *Dogskin* is important primarily for its few superb lyrics and the light it sheds on Auden's other work: the doomed lovers and neurotic society are all there, as are the secret self (Francis Crewe in a dog suit) and the mock-heroic quest; versions of the modern Leader represented onstage by a loudspeaker can also be found in *On the Frontier, For the Time Being* and the more benign *Paul Bunyan*; the Bedlam scene in *Dogskin* prefigures Auden's work in *The Rake's Progress*—in fact, anyone doubting the unity of Auden's *oeuvre* need only consider how often he recycled the same material.

In *The Ascent of F6* (1936), Auden and Isherwood hit on a dramatic structure with the mythic simplicity and resonance of opera. The mountain itself, representing the best and worst human aspirations (as well as its own inhuman immensity), rises above the muddled lives of unknown citizens and the machinations of governments. Michael Ransom, the "truly strong" man, is, like T.E. Lawrence, both inspiring and dangerous. His mountaineering expedition, undertaken partly for nationalistic purposes, is encouraged as well by his mother. It becomes both Ransom's own mystical quest and a nation's ritual sacrifice of its heroes. We see not only the tragic expedition, but also its seriocomic interpretation by the powers below:

> MR. A. [*from stage box*] Why is my work so dull?
>
> GENERAL. That is a most insubordinate remark. Every man has his job in life, and all he has to think about is doing it as well as it can be done. What is needed is loyalty, not criticism. Think of those climbers up on F6. No decent food. No fires. No nice warm beds. Do you think *they* grumble? You ought to be ashamed of yourself.

Ultimately the hero "has died / To satisfy our smug suburban pride," yet by following the struggle on the mountain itself, Auden and Isherwood manage to find some value, too, in the heroic act; Ransom's life has not been entirely wasted, despite its misuse by those who survive him.

Much has been made of Auden's political vision in the thirties, or what he and Isherwood in their "Preliminary Statement" called "The heroic self-immolation of a mistaken society." But their depiction of a bipolar world weirdly anticipates the Cold War era. The last play Auden wrote with Isherwood, *On the Frontier* (1937-38), almost predicts the looking-glass war of John le Carre. *F6* had taught both playwrights the importance of having a visual metaphor in the set. Instead of a mountain, here they have the Ostnia-Westland Room, simultaneously inhabited by two enemy families who are unaware of each other and their nearly identical domestic lives. Auden dramatizes his lifelong obsession with the double man whose public and private selves conflict and pine for impossible unity. The public life is found in the war which devours both nations, the Shavian arms merchant who finds it good business, and the pack of journalists lit like the witches in *Macbeth*. Isherwood had lost his father in World War I, and temporarily so had Auden, while his father was away in the Army. Here they show the devastating private effect of the war on families of both sides. As in his charade, Auden uses a pair of doomed lovers who learn that "We cannot choose our world, our time, our class. None are innocent, none." Finally, as they die, their souls speak with terrible irony of a New Jerusalem:

> ANNA. Europe lies in the dark
> City and flood and tree;
> Thousands have worked and work
> To master necessity.
>
> ERIC. To build the city where
> The will of love is done
> And brought to its full flower
> The dignity of man.
>
> ANNA. Pardon them their mistakes,
> The impatient and wavering will.
> They suffer for our sakes,
> Honour, honour them all.
>
> ERIC. Dry their imperfect dust,
> The wind blows it back and forth.
> They die to make man just
> And worthy of the earth.

This duet could easily be found in an opera; it resembles some that Auden himself was to write. In his introduction to the *Plays*, Mendelson writes, "Against the conscious intent of its author, *On the Frontier* aspired to the condition of opera." I would argue that, despite their wordiness, nearly all of Auden's plays share this perhaps unconscious ambition. It is astonishing now to realize that both *The Ascent of F6* and *On the Frontier* were scored by Benjamin

Britten, for whom Auden would write his first deliberate libretto. Given the success Britten and Auden achieved with individual lyrics and the belated recognition of their operetta, *Paul Bunyan*, I would love to hear the incidental music for these dramas. Mendelson reports that Britten also scored "The Rocking Horse Winner," the 1941 radio play Auden wrote with James Stern. Though the music has been lost, "a tape recording of the play can be obtained through the semi-clandestine market in recordings of radio broadcasts." Mendelson's notes abound in such information.

Paul Bunyan was the only libretto Auden wrote on his own, though before he began it in 1939 he had already fallen in love with his future collaborator, Chester Kallman. Lacking the more dramatic structure of *The Rake's Progress*, *Elegy for Young Lovers* and *The Bassarids*, *Bunyan* is still a delightful piece of musical theatre whose charms should not be underrated. Britten's music, an exuberant mix of folk song, light opera and Broadway show tune, finishes with a fabulous Christmas litany, and Auden's lyrics are as enjoyable as any he ever did (a recording by Phillip Brunelle and the Plymouth Music Series is available from Virgin Classics).

Written at the same time as his long didactic poem, *New Year Letter*, Paul Bunyan celebrates Auden's arrival in the United States, reflects an evolutionary vision of Western culture and meditates on freedom and responsibility in a democracy. The world Auden depicts here is mythical, almost cartoonish, a primordial forest in which "Revolution / Turns to rain" and a Western Union boy can cycle onstage with a telegram from Hollywood. Before Paul arrives, the only conflict we see is that between old and young trees. Then the geese sing of a new agent, man, who "dreams in order to act/And acts in order to dream." Auden has playfully hit on the essence of American aspiration:

> It isn't very often the Conservatives are wrong,
> Tomorrow normally is only yesterday again,
> Society is right in saying nine times out of ten
> Respectability's enough to carry one along.
>
> But once in a while the odd thing happens,
>   Once in a while the dream comes true,
> And the whole pattern of life is altered,
>   Once in a while the Moon turns Blue.

After a mild competition between lumbercamp cooks over the virtues of soup or beans, we encounter the dark side of American freedom; a Quartet of the Defeated sing, "America can break your heart."

Once again, Auden's characters are witty sketches, archetypes rather than full-blown portraits. Johnny Inkslinger is the feckless intellectual in America, forced (somewhat like Christopher Isherwood) to seek his fortune in Hollywood. Hot Biscuit Slim is the heroic tenor whose existential quest for identity occurs only in his introductory song:

> In fair weather and in foul
> Round the world and back,
> I must hunt my shadow
> And the self I lack.

Slim easily surmounts this conflict when he becomes infatuated with Paul's daughter, Tiny, and the two set course for Manhattan to run a hotel. Auden seems to shrug off the obsessions of the thirties, refreshed by a new start in America. Hel Helson's rebellion against Paul in Act Two provides the operetta's only real drama, and it is so quickly dispensed with that the danger hardly registers, yet I've heard the recording a dozen times and seen one live performance, and I continue to find *Paul Bunyan* joyful and moving. More than a musical revue, less than an opera, it's quirky and vibrant and wholly itself. Auden died thinking it a failure, but it's nothing of the sort.

The lack of dramatic conflict was not Auden's only mistake as a beginning librettist. In this published version of *Paul Bunyan*, Mendelson prints a witty love song for Johnny Inkslinger (whose love is for words) and a chorus of Lame Shadows and Animas, which partly explain Auden's falling out with Britten; his verbal play becomes so complex here that a successful setting of the songs is hard to imagine. By the time Auden wrote his great oratorio, *For the Time Being*, which he hoped Britten would score, his wordiness and occasionally overbearing personality had defeated their collaboration. In 1942, Britten returned to England and looked ahead to other projects. Auden stayed on in America, turning his attention to longer poems like *The Sea and the Mirror* and *The Age of Anxiety* and becoming a U.S. citizen in 1946.

When in 1947 Igor Stravinsky decided to compose an opera based on Hogarth's engravings and Auden was recommended (by Aldous Huxley) for the libretto, the poet brought along his protégé, Kallman, and a new partnership was born. Ever the apprentice, Auden had learned from his falling-out with Britten to strive for simplicity in lyrics intended to be set. Together with Kallman, he taught himself a spare dramatic structure suitable for opera, culminating in their radical simplification of Shakespeare for Nicholas Nabokov's *Love's Labour's Lost* (1969).

In conversation with Alan Ansen, Auden had said, "I've decided that opera represents the willful display of emotions. And it's so odd how the characters always manage to fall in love with unsuitable people." *The Rake's Progress*, first performed in Venice in 1951, begins with a hopeful duet and ends in disaster for its two lovers. Tom Rakewell and Anne Trulove are doomed from the start by Rakewell's passive refusal of responsibility:

> Since it is not by merit
> We rise or we fall,
> But the favor of Fortune
> That governs us all,
> Why should I labor
> For what in the end
> She will give me for nothing
> If she be my friend?

Hardly a Don Giovanni, Tom Rakewell is duped into a Faustian bargain without even knowing what he has bargained away; his adversary, Nick Shadow, contrives his ruin in a sequence of scenes corresponding to Hogarth's panels. Auden's most brilliant addition to Hogarth, the outlandish bearded woman Baba the Turk, becomes Tom's wife in Act Two. Rakewell's dissatisfaction is apparent the moment he leaves Anne, but he hasn't got the will to change his life. When he invests in Shadow's fraudulent bread machine, the dream of a mechanical paradise displacing the possibility of love, he hastens his own downfall.

At times Stravinsky's neoclassical score seems cold and detached. The austere melodies of his arias subvert a listener's desire for musical reassurance. Indeed, the emotional energies of the opera are so muted and deflated at its conclusion that ambivalence ensues, like the mistrust of musical forgiveness I alluded to in my opening. We are denied easy pleasures, enjoined by a chorus of madmen to "Leave all love and hope behind." This ending, fitting as it is for Hogarth's satire, is hardly mitigated by a jaunty, Mozartian Epilogue. If Rakewell had possessed Faust's desire for knowledge, if he had used wit to combat Shadow rather than a final game of chance, we might have felt less emptied at the end. Poor Rakewell is hammered by life, never quite knowing why he lived. His final madness is hardly less hopeful than his original love.

Auden reprinted Anne's final barcarolle in *The Shield of Achilles*, a book that concludes with another lyric, "Lauds," taken almost intact from the second libretto Auden and Kallman wrote for Stravinsky, *Delia* (1952). The composer disliked what they had written, and it was never set. Still, it's interesting to compare the quest motif here with that in their 1955 translation and revision of *The Magic Flute*. In *Delia*, the hero Orlando sings,

> O, mine own true love,
>   My vision, then, was true;
> Far, far have I journeyed,
>   Led by a dream of you....

Tamino in *The Magic Flute* sings,

> Dream voices that I could not understand
> Called me and bade me leave my native land:
> By perilous and solitary ways,
> Through forest, fen and desert many days
> My feet have wandered with uncertain aim,
> Driven by longings which I cannot name,
> Seeking I know not what.

What we have here are courtly versions of Hot Biscuit Slim, an Auden type dating back at least to Alan Norman in *The Chase*.

By the 1950s Auden had abandoned drama and the longer poem to focus much of his energy on opera, though there would still be the sequences of poems like "Bucolics," "Horae Canonicae" and "About the House." This is the late period when many critics declared him in decline, but I wonder whether the dissipation of verbal energy in some of Auden's late verse is not somehow related to his apprenticeship to opera. Peter Porter has complained that it is hard for the literary critic to know exactly what to say about the libretti *(TLS,* November 5, 1993). As verse they can seem thin; only with the music added can their full accomplishment be measured. Of the last three major operas in this edition — *Elegy for Young Lovers, The Bassarids* and *Love's Labour's Lost* — I can fairly judge only the second, having heard a good recording of it from the Radio Symphony Orchestra of Berlin. Nevertheless, the libretto of *Elegy* seems, on the page at least, exceedingly strong, especially considering that the story Auden and Kallman devised is completely original.

They met Hans Werner Henze on Ischia in 1953, and five years later he asked them to collaborate with him. Kallman wrote more than half of their new libretto, but many of its preoccupations — the doomed lovers, the dangers of a Romantic poet's egocentricity — seem especially Audenesque. It was Auden who wrote in Act Two, "What the world needs are warmer hearts, / Not older poets." Auden never believed that art was worth the destruction of other peoples' lives; he thought Romantic egotism a prelude to totalitarianism. In their "Genesis of the Libretto," Auden and Kallman wrote that the theme of their opera derived from Yeats' lines: "The intellect of man is forced to choose/Perfection of the life or of the work." Their poet, Gregor Mittenhofer, living on the slopes of his own Parnassus (the F6-like Hammerhorn) is a ruthless genius, a man who sacrifices other people to feed his poetry.

Their next opera, *The Bassarids* (1963), based on Euripides' *The Bacchae,* was even darker and more powerful. Auden's introduction to *The Portable Greek Reader* (1948) had made it clear how deeply he understood the bleak theology of the ancients, and poems like "The Shield of Achilles" linked that vision to a modern political despair. In *Secondary Worlds,* Auden discussed the eighteenth-century belief "that, in a conflict between Reason and Unreason, Reason was bound in the end to be victorious. So in *Die Zauberflöte* the Queen of the Night has a daughter, Pamina; Sarastro acquires a princely disciple, Tamino; the two young innocents fall in love, and the curtain falls upon preparations for their wedding." Euripides' *Bacchae,* he asserts, would hardly have been thought appropriate for opera at that time. But "Today we know only too well that it is as possible for whole communities to become demonically possessed as it is for individuals to go off their heads." Pentheus proves not only the "ungodly man" refusing to worship Dionysus, but a dangerous naif, ignorant of Unreason's all-pervasive power. Henze's music has a violent grandeur (lots of brass), and when Maenads pursue Pentheus we hear a strong rhythm in jazz percussion.

In fact, the opera is so intense that Auden wisely decided to break the tension with a lighter Intermezzo, a miniature eighteenth-century operetta on The Judgement of Calliope (unfortunately missing from my recorded version). When we return to Pentheus' story, he has realized too late the meaning of his own denial:

> I looked into eyes that were my own.
> A full red mouth was rounded on my music.
> It slavered like a bull's
> I was a faceless God
> And worshipped Pentheus.
>
> There stood my grief. It smiled at me.
> My lips were shaped on: *"You shall be forgotten."*
> My front knees dropped. He whispered in my ear:
> "Am I not pure? Say no."
>
> Biting my nape, he drove my flesh away.
>
> [Tearing open his clothes at his chest, with a
> fully conscious cry of desperate grief.]
> No! No! This flesh is me!

The powerful denouement not only has Agave and Cadmus banished, but the Bassarids chillingly singing "Kneel. Adore" while a child smashes her doll at the foot of Semele's tomb. This is terrific opera; I can well understand why Mendelson calls it "the summit of Auden's art as a librettist."

A full appraisal of Auden's vast accomplishment has yet to be made, but the ongoing Princeton edition of *The Complete Works* will make such an appraisal possible for the first time. In that sense, Auden has been extremely well served by his editor and literary executor. Of the radio plays Mendelson has discovered and collected here, at least one, "The Dark Valley" (1940), is a masterpiece, a severe little monologue anticipating Beckett and Pinter, as well as the *The Bassarids*. In it a woman ruminates upon her life and the trouble of freedom while she tries to catch a goose in her yard. The goose, she says, is better off "to have a kind old woman to look after you and feed you and give you a nice coop to live in." The old woman's language is alternately comic, like Herod's in *For the Time Being*, and devastatingly bleak. When she has finished singing "Lady Weeping at the Crossroads" and caught the goose, the old woman sharpens her knife on a grindstone. "I'm sorry," she says, "but it has to be done. Life can't always be pleasant, can it? Geese have to hatch eggs, and grow fat. And old women have to sharpen knives. What for? Why? You may well ask, but who knows? Why are we alive? Why don't we die?"

By the time he wrote these words, Auden had returned to the church, but "The Dark Valley" finds little consolation in religion. He had yet to learn the most difficult lessons of his life from Kallman's betrayal, his mother's death, decades of lonely fame. As he revised his great verse, he grew to mistrust the intoxicating magic of poetry, developing a more casual and prosaic style, but we can be grateful that he never stopped collaborating with others, never stopped pushing himself into longer forms, never abandoned the stage as a public venue for his song.

POSTSCRIPT: THE ESSENTIAL AUDEN FLAW

Years ago I purchased a second-hand paperback copy of *Fore-words and Afterwards*, Edward Mendelson's excellent selection from Auden's prose, and noticed that its previous owner had signed his name inside the cover. This person happens to be a fairly prominent American poet and the editor of a well-known poetry journal; owning his copy gave me such a feeling of conspiratorial pleasure that I neglected to ask myself why he had unloaded it. Some time later I was reading Auden's article, included in the book, on Henry Mayhew's *London Labour and the London Poor*, when I noticed that the previous owner had marked a particular passage in the following paragraph:

> Yet, for all its harrowing descriptions of squalor, crime, injustice and suffering, the final impression of Mayhew's great book is not depressing. From his many transcripts of conversations it is clear that Mayhew was that rare creature, a natural democrat; his first thought, that is to say, was never 'This is an unfortunate wretch whom it is my duty, if possible, to help' but always 'This is a fellow human being whom it is fun to talk to.' The reader's final impression of the London poor is not of their misery but of their self-respect, courage and gaiety in conditions under which it seems incredible that such virtues could survive.

The previous owner had circled the word "fun" and drawn a line to the lower margin, where he had written, "The essential Auden flaw." To the left of the paragraph's final sentence he scrawled, "Immediately covered over."

What could the man have been thinking as he made these notes? In what context could 'fun' be so significant a flaw? How ironic, I thought, that Auden, who had purged his own canon of several beautiful poems because he thought them insufficiently truthful, should now be condemned for his sense of humor. Clearly the American poet and editor who wrote these notes did so out of a perhaps momentary Puritanism, a misguided sobriety dictating that serious subjects like poverty can only be treated seriously. As D. H. Lawrence wrote in *Etruscan Places*, "To the Puritan all things are impure...," and one can imagine the marginalizing critic's anger as he took up his pen. Auden, whose generosity to people like Dorothy Day is well known, stands accused of 'covering over' the facts of poverty's misery when he points out that it might be 'fun' to converse with a person who happens to be poor. My marginalizer apparently believed that the true test of sincerity was a frown, or perhaps a Munchian scream. Taken further, his disapproval explains a lot about post-war American poetry, which at times has elevated the sincere free verse lyric of personal experience over most forms of wit or comedy. The poet's righteousness becomes the subject of poetry, not the suffering world. No wonder Auden is under-appreciated in the United States, where you still meet critics who consider him facile or too cold, as if his delight in traditional forms arose from an indifference to politics.

But what has Auden actually said in his Mayhew piece? He praises Mayhew for treating his subjects as individual human beings, rather than statistics or symbols of social injustice, and he notes that individuals have individual reactions to their own circumstances, whatever those might be. Auden's playful taxonomies (such as his division of human types into Alices and Mabels) are set aside, as are the frustrations with democracy he sometimes displays (e.g. in his preface to Henry James' *The American Scene);* he praises Mayhew for treating the poor as people rather than as types. On the other hand, my marginalizer's view of democracy seems to have been a humorless one, and his dismissal of Auden's article may have led him to unload the book I now possess.

I'm not sure what I can conclude from this small anecdote, except that Auden, who called poetry "a game of knowledge," never failed to see the difference between solutions that are verbal and those that are actually devised in life. Life is always messier than our accounts of it; when we write we order the world, as in a game. Children know that even the worst human experiences, like war, present opportunities for play without actually removing life's dangers. The Puritan who would banish play apparently fears its secular pleasures. If we want to know what Auden understood about suffering, his playful poems will instruct us — and I don't just mean "Musée des Beaux Arts," but also the painful lines of Joseph in *For the Time Being* or the evocations of despair in "The Shield of Achilles" or any number of other works. As Joseph Brodsky has observed, Auden's irony, "this light touch, is the mark of a most profound despair...."

ACHILLES IN THE NO MAN'S LAND

On the first looking into this expensive new edition of the *Iliad*,[1] most readers will wonder whether it is as good as Robert Fitzgerald's translation, which set a contemporary standard in 1974. Fitzgerald was particularly attuned to Homer's world. It was he who wrote, in his "Notes on a Distant Prospect,"

> **I was no more than eight or nine when it had come home to me that the fate of the breathing person was to be hurt and then annihilated.**

But Fitzgerald, who had given us a great *Odyssey*, fell short of the mark in translating the *Iliad*. He missed that poem's savage grandeur, its unalloyed bitterness at human mortality. When in Book Eighteen Achilles cries out despairingly, Fitzgerald lends his cry a possibility—however distant—of melioration. "Ai! let strife and rancor/perish from the lives of gods and men...." Achilles is about to explode violence greater than any we have seen so far in a relentlessly violent poem, but Fitzgerald's version sweetens the bitterness. The new translation by Robert Fagles, on the other hand, responds directly to what is lacking in Fitzgerald. From its very first word—"Rage"—this is a grittier, more fiery version. In the Fagles translation of Book Eighteen, Achilles cries, "If only strife could die from the lives of gods and men," and that reformulation—if only strife *could* die—carries a darker assessment of human nature. The strength of Fagles' translation lies not only in its narrative drive and the power of its best passages, but in its conception, the strongly interpretive line it takes on the meaning of the whole poem. In its almost unmitigated violence, Fagles' version, more than any other I have read, speaks to the bloody history of our century.

Judging a new translation from Homeric Greek is no easy task, especially in an era when few read the language of the original. We can study what Alexander Pope and Matthew Arnold said about Homer's sound. We can wistfully admire the effect of Homer's line on George Seferis, who called it "a vibrating chord," but most of us find this aural paradise inaccessible. Though I have a working knowledge of Modern Greek, I cannot inhabit the archaic language with any feeling of naturalness, and must defer to the studies and reviews of classicists like D. S. Carne-Ross and Rufus Bellamy.

As a rule, though, translation succeeds only if it is to some degree disloyal. Each translation strives, or ought to strive, to be a living work in its own language. It is also an attempted solution to a set of problems, and in the case of Homer one of the problems is what to do about the line. In any narrative poem, the relationship between the story and the line, where enjambment can be used for both lyric and dramatic effects, is crucial. This is why no prose translation can represent a great epic poem. The best translators of Homer have all, to my knowledge, been themselves accomplished poets. Pope's *Iliad* is astonishingly confident and readable; his couplets often seem less intrusive than you might expect. Here, for example, is his graceful opening:

> Achilles' Wrath, to Greece the direful Spring
> Of Woes unnumber'd, heav'nly Goddess, sing!
> That Wrath which hurl'd to *Pluto's* gloomy Reign
> The souls of mighty Chiefs untimely slain;
> Whose Limbs unbury'd on the naked Shore
> Devouring Dogs and hungry Vultures tore.
> Since Great *Achilles* and *Atrides* strove,
> Such was the Sov'reign Doom, and such the Will of *Jove*.

Though his last line has six stresses, Pope makes no attempt to match the unrhymed hexameters of Homer, but chooses a naturalized English line in its Augustan form. (Richmond Lattimore's 1951 translation falls short in part because of its line—a wooden hexameter—and its sometimes stilted diction, whereas Christopher Logue's fragmented versions in *War Music* often seem too campy.) Like Pope, Robert Fitzgerald chose pentameter, but he worked it into supple and various blank verse:

> Anger be now your song, immortal one,
> Akhilleus' anger, doomed and ruinous,
> that caused the Akhaians loss on bitter loss
> and crowded brave souls into the undergloom,
> leaving so many dead men—carrion
> for dogs and birds; and the will of Zeus was done.

This is beautiful work, making good use of fluid vowels, and it has an economy typical of Fitzgerald's best passages. If Homer's line is, as commentators say, both fixed and various, then Pope and Fitzgerald have found useful English equivalents.

Robert Fagles makes an altogether different choice. His basic line is hexameter, but he avoids the rigidity of Lattimore and develops a flexible prosody which nevertheless maintains its formal identity:

> Rage—Goddess, sing the rage of Peleus' son Achilles,
> murderous, doomed, that cost the Achaeans countless losses,
> hurling down to the House of Death so many sturdy souls,
> great fighters' souls, but made their bodies carrion,
> feasts for the dogs and birds,
> and the will of Zeus was moving toward its end.

Seven- and six-beat lines establish a loose pattern (the last line is pentameter, which is also used frequently in the text), and Fagles adopts the blank verse variation of Shakespeare and Milton when he pulls back to trimeter. His six opening lines are more unruly than Fitzgerald's, but also more muscular. His "Rage" has more force than Fitzgerald's "Anger" or Pope's "Wrath." He even does a better job of distinguishing the souls of the fighters, the life-breath that will be robbed from so many of them, from the carrion their bodies will become.

Fagles is careful to pay homage to Fitzgerald in his preface, and at times Fitzgerald's version remains the superior one; his rendering of Trojan grief at the end of Book Twenty-Two, for example, is more economical than Fagles'. But Fitzgerald is often too elegant, choosing a Latinate word where Fagles will choose an Anglo-Saxon one, and in consequence his *Iliad* touches its spilled blood with greater delicacy. Fagles plunges both fists into the gore; he mucks about in it. In Book Ten he makes the vacated battlefield so gruesome that he reminds me of *All Quiet on the Western Front*. When the Achaeans extract a confession from Dolon, a Trojan spy, and Odysseus stands back while pitiless Diomedes beheads their prisoner, Fagles writes,

> ...Diomedes struck him square across the neck—
> a flashing hack of the sword—both tendons snapped
> and the shrieking head went tumbling in the dust.

Fitzgerald's version of the same passage is comparatively passive: "In the dust / the head of the still crying man was muffled."

Men die more horribly in the new translation. Guts uncoil and spill; brains splatter inside helmets. The deaths themselves are the same — as are Homer's famous similes when killing is compared to a harvest or a fisherman gaffing his catch — but Fagles' diction more often carries the awful sounds of hacking, screaming and clawing the earth. Homer is so inventive when it comes to fatal wounds (Agamemnon slashes off one man's arms, lops off his head, and sends him "rolling through the carnage like a log") that one can imagine an audience laughing grimly as each new death surpasses the last. But when we expect the killing to stop and it doesn't, when the lists of dead read like a ghoulish parody of Biblical begats, the horror is overwhelming, as it is certainly meant to be.

Fagles is more likely than most other translators to use modern historical diction, referring at one point to "Trojan shock troops"; the battlefield becomes a "no man's land" where fallible heroes prepare for "Total war." Even wise old Nestor exults in the slaughter: "Now's the time for killing! Later, at leisure, I strip the corpses up and down the plain!" When Achilles insults Agamemnon in Book Nine, Fagles relishes the invective and indulges in a violent pun about Briseis — "enjoy her to the hilt!" — that Fitzgerald does not give us.

Because of Fagles' talent for bitter language, one might expect him to do less well with the lyrical set pieces which leaven the poem's horror, but even in many of these he writes beautifully. When, near the end of Book Seven, the dead of both sides are cremated, Fitzgerald buries the lovely passage within a long column of verse, but Fagles gives it a moving stanza of its own:

> Just as the sun began to strike the plowlands,
> rising out of the deep calm flow of the Ocean River
> to climb the vaulting sky, the opposing armies met.
> And hard it was to recognize each man, each body,
> with clear water they washed the clotted blood away
> and lifted them onto wagons, weeping warm tears.
> Priam forbade his people to wail aloud. In silence
> they piled the corpses on the pyre, their hearts breaking,
> burned them down to ash and returned to sacred Troy.

And just so on the other side Achaean men-at-arms
piled the corpses on the pyre, their hearts breaking,
burned them down to ash and returned to the hollow ships.

These lines are simple and powerful (Fitzgerald misses the opportunity to make the Achaean ships "hollow"). The tragic tone of the *Iliad* derives from our knowledge that all joys are brief, and no one, not even Achilles, escapes death. Men strive for honor and glory (and Helen, too, becomes sympathetic in her self-knowledge), but death in Homer's world is utterly unconsoling. The *Iliad* gives us figures who are desperately alive; they cling to what pleasures they have or can recall because death is a nothingness, an absence — annihilation.

At times Fagles' line slackens too much, and in a few passages, such as the death of Asius in Book Thirteen, a proliferation of pronouns makes it difficult to tell who is butchering whom. If Fagles really intends to transform Homer's Greek into a modern English poem, he ought to be able to solve these problems (Pope is the only translator I have read who renders the death of Asius with complete clarity). Some readers may also object to Fagles' use of Greek proper names in their old Latinized spellings. Fitzgerald created phonetic transliterations, giving his text an Hellenic look and sound, but he also complicated reading for anyone who cannot imagine what that sound might be like. Fagles has found a workable compromise, though it constantly reminds us of our distance from the original language.

These are small complaints to raise about so mammoth an endeavor. Though Fagles has published numerous translations and an interesting book of his own poems based on the words and paintings of Van Gogh, these accomplishments don't prepare you for the poetic successes of his *Iliad*. In addition, the book at hand is handsomely bound and printed, with some helpful notes and a thorough, eloquent introduction by Bernard Knox.

At it best, Fagles' translation convinces me that I had not previously understood the richness and contemporary value of the poem. I am struck once again by Homer's psychological complexity: heroes sob and shrink; Hector's son, Astyanax, screams at the sight of his father fresh from battle; Nestor longs for his youthful prowess, then wonders if it wasn't all a dream; Achilles fumes, first in hurt pride ("... that man has no intention of quenching his rage," Odysseus says), then in hopeless grief; a grieving Priam lashes out at his surviving sons; Achilles and Priam weep together, two mortal enemies bound in a precarious moment of sympathy, and on the next page Achilles nearly loses patience with the old man. No wonder the god Apollo is perplexed by human behavior:

> "... this Achilles—first he slaughters Hector,
> he rips away the noble prince's life
> then lashes him to his chariot, drags him round
> his beloved comrade's tomb. But why, I ask you?
> What good will it do him? What honor will he gain?
> Let that man beware, or great and glorious as he is,
> we mighty gods will wheel on him in anger—look,
> he outrages the senseless clay in all his fury!"

The gods have already wheeled on Achilles. He knows full well that he is doomed, and chooses to die speedily. The fickleness of the gods only dramatizes inscrutable nature, and their occasional pity may be nothing more than humanity's wishful reading of their absence.

Where we stand on the *Iliad* has much to do with where we stand on hope or hopelessness. If we believe in the possibility of permanent world peace, we might well find this epic outworn and overlong. But if we believe that strife is in our natures, that we are doomed to struggle against each other and ourselves, the *Iliad* will speak to us like nothing else.

[1] A review of *The Iliad*, translated by Robert Fagles.

A TOUCHSTONE FROM TENNYSON

Words can assume a personal significance beyond their lexical identities; they are saturated with private associations. My grandfather's name was Abraham—a fact I do not take lightly. He was a candy-maker in Trinidad, Colorado, and as a result most of my early memories of him are sweet. When I grew older and learned more about my family's wanderlust, what became significant about Abe was not only his symbolic position at the head of a peripatetic tribe, but also the fact that the brown river flowing through his town was called —no doubt by French trappers—the Purgatoire. Suddenly Old and New Testament associations ran together in the history of my clan. And before the French, a party of Spanish conquistadors had first called the river *El Rio de las Animas Perdidas en Purgatorio*, so I have been free to imagine my family as a tribe of lost souls.

I learned much of this years ago at a family reunion held near a rock formation called Stonewall Gap. Like many Americans, I have my genealogical obsessions, and I saved all the family documents I was given at this gathering. Leafing through old xeroxes of apparently unrelated data, I discovered yet another complicated connection: this time between my family and the poems of Alfred, Lord Tennyson.

My grandfather's grandfather was also named Abraham; he was born in Kentucky in 1824, and died in Paris, Missouri, in 1887, "aged 62 years, 5 months and 5 days," according to his obituary. This document is quite detailed, perhaps because my ancestor had edited the paper in which it appeared, the Paris *Mercury*. There is a lengthy biography and description of the obsequies, concluding as follows:

> To his deeply afflicted and sorrowing wife and children we tender our deepest sympathy, trusting that a kind and loving providence will ever watch and tend them as they journey on in life.

> The stately ships go on,
> To their haven under the hill,
> But oh for the touch of a vanished hand
> And the sound of a voice that is still.

There is a bit more—what a gentleman he was, "so true to the high moral principles that should prevail throughout the country," and so forth. But notice the Tennyson. Notice, among other things, the little misquotations, suggesting that the writer worked from memory. "Lawn Tennyson," as James Joyce would later call him, was still very much alive and writing when his poem "Break, break, break," was misquoted in Abraham Mason's obituary. In short, Tennyson was exceedingly famous, known by heart wherever English was spoken. In 1883 he had been elevated to a peerage, and each of his publications was an event noted on several continents, but apparently he was not yet resented as a voice of Empire.

This fame and popularity, as well as the sentimentality of his worst poems, resulted in Tennyson's dismissal by a great many twentieth century critics—even those, like T. S. Eliot, who were influenced by him. Though Eliot would later write an admiring introduction to *In Memoriam*, his often-quoted remarks in "The Metaphysical Poets" seem to have stuck firmly in the minds of many critics:

> Tennyson and Browning are poets, and they think; but they do not feel their thought as immediately as the odour of a rose. A thought to Donne was an experience; it modified his sensibility.

When he adds, slightly later, that "Keats and Shelley died" while "Tennyson and Browning ruminated," he seems to view Victorian poetry as a diminished thing. The power of such dismissals was so strong that I avoided reading Tennyson for years, until I heard a reading of "Break, Break, Break" that moved me to go back to his poems. There I discovered a master of verse technique and a poet of great feeling, a figure I was unwilling to dismiss, in whose poems I still take unguilty pleasure.

When I teach poetry, I often use this little poem as an example of the power inherent in meter. Here is the whole of the well-known text:

> Break, break, break,
>   On thy cold gray stones, O Sea!
> And I would that my tongue could utter
>   The thoughts that arise in me.

O well for the fisherman's boy
    That he shouts with his sister at play!
O well for the sailor lad,
    That he sings in his boat on the bay!

And the stately ships go on
    To their haven under the hill;
But O for the touch of a vanished hand,
    And the sound of a voice that is still!

Break, break, break,
    At the foot of thy crags, O Sea!
But the tender grace of a day that is dead
    Will never come back to me.

Students first learning the technique of scansion are driven mad by this poem. They are used to the predominance of iambic and other two-syllable feet in English poetry, and their scansions of Victorians, for whom three-syllable feet were perfectly natural, are often hilarious. Some are tempted to find exotic fauna like the molossus (a three-syllable foot with every syllable long or stressed) in the poem's first line. Students who have studied music usually hear right away what the pattern is—a simple three feet per line, usually with three firmly stressed syllables. I could scan the first stanza as follows:

> 3 monosyllabic feet
>   anapest, spondee, iamb
> 2 anapests and an amphybrach
>   iamb, anapest, iamb

The second foot of line two could also be an iamb, depending on which side of the bed you got up on this morning.

Now, several fascinating technical matters occur to me when I read this poem. First, it is an example of verse in which a great many three-syllable feet, usually anapests, do not create the galloping rhythm so famously illustrated in Byron's "The Destruction of Sennacherib." Where Byron's poem is regularly anapestic, Tennyson's contains a variety of two and three-syllable feet. Second, the repetition of the opening line at the start of the final stanza has a braking—as well as breaking—effect, slowing the poem down. Finally, Tennyson's significant variations have emotional effects. The fact that the third lines in stanzas three and four are the poem's only tetrameters becomes crucial; read the poem aloud, and you will hear that the first of these occurs at the poem's emotional crux: "But O for the touch of a vanished hand...." When Tennyson alters his meter and extends the line, he breaks your heart.

This sort of controlled variety almost disappears in the twentieth century, and ought to be brought back by our most capable poets. Many of the New Formalists in America have been too easily satisfied with the thumping iamb; they might do well to study Tennyson's meter-making moods. No doubt some readers find this poem sentimental. I find it a simple expression of memorable emotion, achieved with what appears to have been near-spontaneous mastery, the inner condition of the poet presented in images of the external world and in telling cadences. As the Victorian critic R.H. Hutton wrote, "No poet ever made the dumb speak so effectually."

I said earlier that I had avoided reading Tennyson for years, under the influence of modernist critics, or especially the influence of teachers swayed by such critics. The event that lured me back to him was a memorial service for my older brother, Douglas Cameron Mason, who died in a mountaineering accident just short of his twenty-ninth birthday in 1979. The service was held in Seattle, where my brother had lived and engaged in politics. An old family friend, Marshall Forrest, a judge in both state and local courts, built his fine eulogy around Tennyson's poem. Years later, I would notice the obituary for our great-great grandfather, quoting—or misquoting—the same verses. It felt as if a circle had closed. I had been given another example of the deep connections between life and art. Perhaps these connections are coincidence, but when they instruct us as this one did me, coincidences resonate throughout our experience.

As readers of poetry, we all have our touchstones, poems we come back to without always knowing why. Sometimes life appears to choose these poems for us and we have to learn how to love them, even when they might embarrass us among our intellectual friends.

We learn where our loyalties lie by listening for the truth.

AMERICAN POETRY IN THE NINETEENTH CENTURY

I hear a river thro' the valley wander
Whose water runs, the song alone remaining...
— Trumbull Stickney

A few years ago, driving the back roads of Nebraska, my wife and I stopped in a small town so faded and neglected that its cemetery seemed livelier than its streets. Outside the town we discovered, in a hen-pecked yard full of junked appliances and old cars, a second-hand shop in a trailer. While my wife sought out old photographs, I fingered dusty books and magazines. My bittersweet purchase that day was a series of small pamphlets, *Classical Poems*, printed for Grades One through Eight by Stephenson School Supply Company in Lincoln. They are slender enough to fit in a jacket pocket, and though they bear no copyright date, a fair guess would be that they were used sometime in the mid-twentieth century.

These pamphlets remain on my desk, reminding me that poetry has served the everyday lives of schoolchildren in this country, that possibly our schools once expected more knowledge of poetry than they do now. First graders were treated not only to verses by Robert Louis Stevenson and Christina Rossetti but to a battery of Mother Goose Rhymes, Longfellow's "Snowflakes" and "Hiawatha's Childhood," Eugene Field's "Little Boy Blue," and a curiosity called "Indian Children" by Annette Wynne:

> Where we walk to school each day
>   Indian children used to play—
> All about our native land,
>   Where the shops and houses stand.
>
> And the trees were very tall,
>   And there were not streets at all,
> Not a church and not a steeple—
>   Only woods and Indian people.
>
> Only wigwams on the ground,
>   And at night bears prowling round.
> What a different place today
>   Where we live and work and play!

There are many reasons why these verses might not be given to American children now; but, whether in innocence or ignorance, they allude to a tenuousness at the heart of a mighty nation, misgivings implicit even in the celebration of Christian and commercial culture.

Eighth-grade readers of my pocket anthologies were expected to respond to far more complicated fare: poets like Burns, Keats, Shelley, Browning, Tennyson, and Kipling (the uplifting "If") side by side with a variety of Americans like Arthur Guiterman, William Cullen Bryant, Hamlin Garland, Emily Dickinson, Oliver Wendell Holmes, Edgar Allan Poe, Ralph Waldo Emerson, James Russell Lowell, and Henry Wadsworth Longfellow. None of the poems included would upset a conservative school board, but only readers of some sophistication could appreciate them—readers I suspect we would be hard-pressed to find in our high schools today. These were celebrated nineteenth-century poets, their work still popular well into our century. A few of them are among the ablest writers our country has produced, yet their audience seems to have vanished in those tidy roadside cemeteries. I don't begrudge the inevitable change, but I wonder whether American poetry will ever again find so portable a form or be so commonly a part of schoolchildren's lives.

Of course poetry remains surprisingly vital—in bars and coffee shops as well as classrooms—but one doesn't have to be a rigid traditionalist to lament the altered culture of reading. In both cafes and classrooms, poetry is often presented as though it were only social commentary or ideology or an alternative therapy. When we talk of the nineteenth century, we usually refer only to two great poets, their names melding into one—Whitman Dickinson—as if the whole century were defined by a single schizophrenic, at once robust and retiring, the marginalized pansexual and the neglected woman. Whitman and Dickinson are often discussed in ideological or psychological terms—the psychology becoming ideology and approved by academic gatherings. In his recently published lectures, *Writing Was Everything*, Alfred Kazin rages at contemporary academic critics for their manner of reading and discussing literature:

> At a Modern Language Association convention in 1989—the session was called "The Muse of Masturbation," and it was thronged—it was noted that the hidden strategy of Emily Dickinson's

poetry is her use of "encoded images of clitoral masturbation to transcend sex-role limitations imposed by the 19th century patriarchy."
The basic idea was that Dickinson loaded her work with references
to peas, crumbs, and flower buds in order to broadcast secret mes-
sages of forbidden onanistic delights to other female illuminati. "Why
does she write in such short, explosive sentences?" the speaker asked.
"The style is clitoral, as far as I'm concerned."

By contrast the schoolchildren who grew up with my pamphlets
would have understood intuitively that Dickinson's style—simultaneously experimental and rooted in her time—has more to do
with poetry itself. The rhythms of verse are much more than a form
of discourse; they are a way of living in language, of holding experience in both broad and memorable terms. Poetry is not only, as
Frost said, what gets lost in translation; it is also rapidly becoming
what gets lost in criticism and the classroom. The culture of reading has been wholly transformed in just a few generations.

That is why John Hollander's magnificent two-volume anthology *American Poetry: The Nineteenth Century* (Library of America,
1993), is such an important contribution to the literary life of the
nation. Hollander reminds us of the great variety of our poetry.
Whitman and Dickinson remain the dominant figures they in many
ways deserve to be; but Hollander does not forget the contributions of Longfellow, Poe, Melville, Bryant, Whittier, and others;
and he includes a range of medium or smaller accomplishment, of
poets who may have produced a few good poems, but whose talent
has been neglected by recent anthologists. In addition Hollander
delights in eccentricities: the comedians and anthem writers, two
Presidents and at least one Secretary of State who wrote verse, the
transcribers of Indian pictographs and chants, the spirituals,
worksongs, and folk poetry that made up so much of our nation's
consciousness. By letting the great poets coexist with their lesser
contemporaries, Hollander in his anthology restores the century to
us as no other recent book has done.

It was, one might say, the true century of our founding. The
nation was tested to its anxious roots by migration, emigration,
civil war, and embryonic civil-rights movements. National pride
and unrest, hope and cynicism, run through these poems, as well
as a new animism inspired by what Longfellow called "the forest

primeval," a clapboard Christianity confronting or dodging its own limits, all of it marked by a knowledge of received forms. A doubting resilience underlay utilitarian and spiritual convictions. The nation was new and nostalgic at the same time. I mean "nostalgia" in its root sense, as a pain or melancholy deriving from an absence from home. Americans were building and regretting from the start. One can see this in the romanticism of Philip Freneau:

> Go, teach what Reason dictates should be taught,
> And learn from *Indians* one great Truth you ought,
> That, through the world, wherever man exists,
> Involved in darkness, or obscured in mists,
> The *Negro*, scorching on *Angola's* coasts,
> Or *Tartar*, shivering in *Siberian* frosts;
> Take all, through all, through nation, tribe, or clan,
> The child of Nature is the *better* man.

These august (nearly Augustan) couplets express ideas learned both from Rousseau and from the New World itself. Freneau was educated at the College of New Jersey (which would become Princeton University). He fought in the American Revolution, suffered aboard a British prison ship, championed the French Revolution, worked in Jefferson's government and later as a journalist, and, like so many American writers, ended his days in poverty. Freneau died of exposure while walking home during a blizzard (many of these biographical details come from the marvelous notes appearing in the back of Hollander's volumes).

Specialists in nineteenth-century American literature know all this and more, but amateurs like myself will find Hollander's volumes packed with surprises. For example I had known of Thomas Cole chiefly for his landscapes from the Hudson River Valley and his four allegorical paintings called *The Voyage of Life*. But Cole was also a poet. In "The Lament of the Forest" he praises the great age of Nature in Arcadian terms, and frets about the coming of civilization:

> Then all was harmony and peace; but MAN
> Arose—he who now vaunts antiquity—
> He the destroyer—and in the sacred shades
> Of the far East began destruction's work.

When Cole departed for the obligatory trip to the artistic capitals of Europe, his friend William Cullen Bryant provided a sonnet to remind him of the country he was leaving behind:

> Lone lakes—savannahs where the bison roves—
>> Rocks rich with summer garlands—solemn streams—
>> Skies, where the desert eagle wheels and screams—
> Spring bloom and autumn blaze of boundless groves.

Bryant, whose career was long and successful, would be on hand to deliver the funeral oration for Cole in 1848, an honor he would later perform for Washington Irving as well.

Among nature poets Bryant is remarkable because so much of his career developed in cities like New York and Washington. Editor-in-chief of the New York *Evening Post* from 1829 until his death in 1878, Bryant lived a life of public triumph. In 1860 he introduced Abraham Lincoln at Cooper Union; four years later, at seventy, he was treated to a festival in his honor at the Century Club. He traveled widely, knew almost everybody, and died in the midst of all this social activity. His two most famous poems, "Thanatopsis" and "To a Waterfowl," were composed when he was only twenty years old. "Go forth, under the open sky," he wrote in the former, "and list/To Nature's teachings." He never forgot his pastoral roots, fed on Spenser, Milton, and Wordsworth. Poem after poem takes for its situation a walk in the woods, and one rarely glimpses the hectic life from which he sought relief, though "Autumn Woods" concludes with some sense of it:

> Ah! 'twere a lot too blest
> Forever in thy colored shades to stray;
> Amidst the kisses of the soft southwest
> To rove and dream for aye;
>
> And leave the vain low strife
> That makes men mad—the tug for wealth and power,
> The passions and the cares that wither life,
> And waste its little hour.

Bryant's tutored pastoralism (so much in tune with English Romanticism) would find its counterpart in one of the roughs, Walt Whitman, as early as 1855:

> I think I could turn and live awhile with the
>   animals . . . they are so placid and self-contained,
> I stand and look at them sometimes half the day long.
>
> They do not sweat and whine about their condition,
> They do not lie awake in the dark and weep for their sins,
> They do not make me sick discussing their duty to God,
> Not one is dissatisfied.... Not one is demented with the mania of
>   owning things,
> Not one kneels to another nor to his kind that lived
>   thousands of years ago,
> No one is respectable or industrious over the whole earth.

Whatever one thinks of Whitman's poetry as *poetry*, it is easy to see why readers from Swinburne to Edwin Arlington Robinson found him a blast of fresh air.

One might say of Bryant that he gave us conventional thinking in conventional language, but in his best poems the language is so gorgeous that it pulses with meditative life. He was particularly good at blank verse. A rhymed poem like "An Indian at the Burying-Place of his Fathers," however appropriate its subject (the desecration of holy ground by unthinking whites), put what now seems highly inappropriate diction in the mouth of its Indian speaker:

> Methinks it were a nobler sight
>   To see these vales in woods arrayed,
> Their summits in the golden light,
>   Their trunks in grateful shade,
> And herds of deer, that bounding go
> O'er hills and prostrate trees below.

I can imagine Bugs Bunny, that withering critic, making light of lines like these. Yet poets who wrote about Indians—Freneau, Bryant, and Lydia Huntley Sigourney among many others—were after a fundamental truth about the land they inhabited. There is indeed a sacredness in Adam's naming task, and white Americans found themselves in a landscape that had already been named; many of those names survive into the present day. Even a city dweller like Bryant could not escape the origins of "Manhattan." American civilization was born of a great anxiety about civilization itself. The nobility of nature and those close to nature had a wealth of Old World precedents, dating back at least to Theocritus, if not earlier, but to many Americans this nobility would have seemed self-evident by virtue of the forests, prairies, and mountains that confronted them. Our most cultivated writers have often been ambivalent, to say the least, about high culture. Our heroes are often untutored men, from the frontiersman to the football star.

One of the most popular poems of the nineteenth century, Whittier's "Snow-Bound," is a case in point. In lovely tetrameter couplets Whittier indulges himself in the purest nostalgia, the "Angel of the backward look," and portrays a family snowbound for a week in that family's New England home. They seem by and large a well-adjusted lot, and some of their virtue comes from their closeness to the land:

> Our uncle, innocent of books,
> Was rich in lore of fields and brooks,
> The ancient teachers never dumb
> Of Nature's unhoused lyceum.

The poem appeared in 1866 to great acclaim, and earned Whittier a fortune. In the same year Herman Melville published his far less nostalgic verses on the Civil War, a book that received mixed reviews and deeply disappointed its author by its lackluster sales. Yet Whittier's success was not wholly owing to sentimentality: he touched a domestic nerve in his readers, but his poem is about the loss of such tranquillity, the advent of change brought on by the war and time's passage. Whittier describes a by-gone family life that many of his readers would have known or hoped for:

> So days went on: a week had passed
> Since the great world was heard from last.
> The Almanac we studied o'er,
> Read and reread our little store,
> Of books and pamphlets, scarce a score;
> One harmless novel, mostly hid
> From younger eyes, a book forbid,

And poetry, (good or bad,
A single book was all we had,)
Where Ellwood's meek, drab-skirted Muse,
    A stranger to the heathen Nine,
    Sung, with a somewhat nasal whine,
The wars of David and the Jews.
At last the floundering carrier bore
The village paper to our door.
Lo! broadening outward as we read,
To warmer zones the horizon spread;
In panoramic length unrolled
We saw the marvels that it told.

"Snow-Bound" is full of charm, a quality we should not underrate, and is marked with perfect touches like that paper carrier floundering in the snow.

Whittier's poetry is vivid and accessible. At times he displays a clear sense of what we might once have called "the American character," and what some still hold as a democratic ideal:

    Yet here at least an earnest sense
Of human right and weal is shown;
    A hate of tyranny intense,
    And hearty in its vehemence,
As if my brother's pain and sorrow were my own.

This work, "'Proem," ends with an exclamation not far removed from the exaltations of Whitman, and in "My Triumph" one sees a visionary impulse akin to "Crossing Brooklyn Ferry." Like Bryant, Whittier was greatly celebrated in his long life (1807-1892); perhaps his popularity has lowered his reputation among certain critics, but he was not by any means a simple-minded writer. A modern reader may wince at the nationalism of "Barbara Frietchie," forgetting the national crisis that created such heroic pride.

Indeed the neglect of some popular poets stems partly from a narrowing perception of what poetry can be, beginning with the dismissal of certain formal and syntactical strategies by the modernists, and perpetuated by our contemporaries, for whom poetry and prose are often interchangeable terms. Twentieth-century critics have usually prized difficulty and realism above all other qualities, and few have been willing or able to make the historical adjustments necessary to appreciate popular poets of the past.

Perhaps no major poet of the nineteenth century has suffered more at the hands of modern critics than Longfellow, as Dana Gioia demonstrates in a long essay collected in *The Columbia History of American Poetry* (published in 1993, the same year that gave us Hollander's anthology): "In intellectual discourse that valorizes indeterminacy, self-referentiality and deconstruction, Longfellow's aesthetic has more in common with that of Virgil or Ovid than with the assumptions of Beckett or Ashbery. But unlike Virgil and Ovid, who today exist solely as objects of academic study, Longfellow refuses to stay in the tiny cell critics have afforded him. He can still be sighted—to the scholar's embarrassment—prowling at large in the general culture."

The same can be said of a poet like Whittier; one of my colleagues, a man now in his fifties, recalls his working-class mother reciting "Snow-Bound" to him when he was a boy. But Longfellow's accomplishment is vaster than those of either Whittier or Bryant. More fluid and accessible than Emerson or Melville, Longfellow is also among the most varied of our poets. His metrical diversity rivals that of Tennyson.

I notice the confidence of his technique in a passage like the following from "The Spirit of Poetry," where one line-break creates a surprising moment of assonance:

> ...Blue skies, and silver clouds, and gentle winds,—
> The swelling upland, where the sidelong sun
> Aslant that wooded slope, at evening, goes,—
> Groves, through whose broken roof the sky looks in...

That near rhyme of "goes" and "Groves" is matched in the poem's final two lines: "the rich music of a summer bird,/Heard in the still night, with its passionate cadence."

Gioia acknowledges the sentimentality in lyrics like "A Psalm of Life," but what poets are without their flaws? Longfellow's flaws hardly warrant his dismissal from the canon. A popular poem like "The Wreck of the Hesperus" builds on the ballad tradition of "Sir Patrick Spens," and it contains striking images:

The breakers were right beneath her bows,
    She drifted a dreary wreck,
And a whooping billow swept the crew
    Like icicles from her deck.

To derive pleasure from poems like these, one must not only have
the historical sense Gioia mentions; one must also recover the innocent delight in reading that drew us to poetry in the first place.
When we condemn the clichés of a Tennyson or Longfellow, we
reject only what subsequent writers have overused. A modern poet
writing of "the corridors of Time" might be laughed out of his workshop, but the phrase is not so pitiful in the context of Longfellow's
poem "The Day is Done":

Come, read to me some poem,
    Some simple and heartfelt lay,
That shall soothe this restless feeling,
    And banish the thoughts of day.

Not from the grand old masters,
    Not from the bards sublime,
Whose distant footsteps echo
    Through the corridors of Time.

For, like strains of martial music,
    Their mighty thoughts suggest
Life's endless toil and endeavor;
    And to-night I long for rest.

Read from some humbler poet,
    Whose songs gushed from his heart,
As showers from the clouds of summer,
    Or tears from the eyelids start;

Who, through long days of labor,
    And nights devoid of ease,
Still heard in his soul the music
    Of wonderful melodies.

Such songs have the power to quiet
   The restless pulse of care,
And come like the benediction
   That follows after prayer.

Then read from the treasured volume
   The poem of thy choice,
And lend to the rhyme of the poet
   The beauty of thy voice.

And the night shall be filled with music,
   And the cares, that infest the day,
Shall fold up their tents, like the Arabs,
   And silently steal away.

A weak phrase like "wonderful melodies" or the stereotyping of Arabs would be enough to banish this poem from most current academic discussions, while another poem, "The Jewish Cemetery at Newport," can no longer be read as Longfellow's first readers might have taken it, because modern history has complicated our reading.

Longfellow is not always simple or sentimental, of course. The emotions contained in his lyrics are often complex, as in the Dantean sonnet "Mezzo Cammin," or late lyrics like "The Cross of Snow," "The Tide Rises, the Tide Falls" and "Night." All this is to say nothing of Longfellow's formal experiments, the dactylic hexameters of *Evangeline* or the trochaic tetrameters of *The Song of Hiawatha*. (I once heard the Irish poet Gabriel Rosenstock recite a long passage from the latter work to illustrate the intoxicating sounds that first drew him to poetry.) Longfellow's narrative poems anticipate those of Frost, and at times, especially in *Evangeline*, they achieve the grandeur we can find in Whitman and Jeffers. But Frost was also indebted to Longfellow's lyrics, taking the title of his first book from "My Lost Youth." If, as W. H. Auden contended, Frost was more Prospero than Ariel, more earthbound than spritely, Longfellow gives us equal measures of realism and *poesie pure*.

Since the current elevation of Whitman and Dickinson obscures other fine poets of their time, I will pass lightly over their works, which together take up 335 pages in Hollander's anthology (Longfellow gets 80, fewer than either Emerson or Melville). Both of these poets, so expansive in vision, are rather limited where formal technique is concerned, yet both achieve a kind of verbal alertness startling even today. In Dickinson's case I doubt that her greatness has much to do with her private life, except to the degree that the life informed the vivid accuracy of her poems. Her mind moves from blossom to blossom like a bee, and the action of the mind in its apprehension of the world is quite often her subject. Almost a feminine Hamlet, she can be too self-absorbed and fretful; but there is also, as with the Danish prince, an attractive resilience and humor. Ultimately she passes the test that matters most for a poet: she creates unforgettable verses. Hollander does not include what is for me one of her finest poems about her favorite subject — death:

> The Bustle in a House
> The Morning after Death
> Is solemnest of industries
> Enacted upon Earth—
>
> The Sweeping up the Heart,
> And putting Love away
> We shall not want to use again
> Until Eternity.

"Hearth" becomes 'heart," the common activity both containing and unable to contain our most profound emotions.

Whitman is *sui generis*. It is useless to complain with purists about his excesses when the broad embrace is so welcome and welcoming. "O Christ!" he exclaims in "Song of Myself." "My fit is mastering me!" We might too easily conclude that old notions of mastery will no longer serve. If his lack of restraint becomes boring at times, it also produces a vulgar majesty capable of inspiring awe. When he shrugs off his own contradictions, or when he writes that "copulation is no more rank to me than death is," he becomes the voice of liberality. He knew what a sham he could be, obsessed with "the life that exhibits itself" even when he tried to escape it, yet the particularity of his compassion was extraordinary. After reading Melville's Civil War poems, for example, one is shocked to return to Whitman's images:

From the stump of the arm, the amputated hand,
I undo the clotted lint, remove the slough, wash
      off the matter and blood,
Back on his pillow the soldier bends with curv'd neck
      and side-falling head,
His eyes are closed, his face is pale, he dares not
      look on the bloody stump,
And has not yet look'd on it.

I dress a wound in the side, deep, deep,
But a day or two more, for see the frame all wasted
      and sinking,
And the yellow-blue countenance see.

I dress a perforated shoulder, the foot with the
      bullet wound,
Cleanse the one with a gnawing and putrid gangrene,
      so sickening, so offensive,
While the attendant stands behind aside me
      holding the tray and pail.

I am faithful, I do not give out,
The fractured thigh, the knee, the wound
      in the abdomen,
These and more I dress with impassive hand, (yet
      deep in my breast a fire, a burning flame.)

Even in such powerful moments we can be aware of the self-ag-grandizing poet, the egotistical attempt at honesty that resurfaces in confessional poets like Robert Lowell, Sylvia Plath, and Anne Sexton. But Whitman had a gigantic view; he was able to take in the hope and griefs of the whole nation, as he does in the almost-homeric poem "Reconciliation":

Word over all, beautiful as the sky,
Beautiful that war and all its deeds of carnage
      must in time be utterly lost,

That the hands of the sisters Death and Night
     incessantly softly wash again, and ever
     again, this soil'd world;
For my enemy is dead, a man divine as myself is dead,
I look where he lies white-faced and still in the
     coffin—I draw near,
Bend down and touch lightly with my lips the white
     face in the coffin.

If Whitman's excesses usually burst the confines of meter, the rolling free verse he invented (with the help of the King James Bible and other sources) returns to meter in many of his most memorable passages. In fact "Reconciliation" can be recomposed in lines of rough blank verse:

Word over all, beautiful as the sky,
Beautiful that war and all its deeds
Of carnage must in time be utterly lost,
That the hands of the sisters Death and Night
Incessantly softly wash again, and ever
Again, the soil'd world; for my enemy is dead,
A man divine as myself is dead, I look
Where he lies white-faced and still in the coffin—
I draw near, bend down and touch lightly with my lips
The white face in the coffin.

I could scan those lines using a liberal mix of two- and three-syllable feet, proving that Whitman's free verse moves in and out of meter. His most memorable free verse is often his most measured; Whitman is modern not only in his attitudes, but in his use of both prose and verse techniques (though we should remember that Shakespeare and Blake did the same thing in their own ways).

Among other poets who seized the Civil War as a subject, Herman Melville has been until recently little appreciated. Robert Penn Warren, who edited a fine selection of Melville's verse (1970), wrote in the introduction to that volume: "In a very profound way it can be said that the Civil War made Melville a poet." In *The Civil War World of Herman Melville* (1993), Stanton Garner charts both the despair and the deliberation with which Melville followed events, turning them into poems that were composed mostly after the fall of Richmond. Though not as graphic as Whitman's, Melville's war poems are just as visionary. Both poets shared Lincoln's view that the war had become the nation's terrible rebirth. *Moby-Dick* is often cited for its poetic passages, some of which can be scanned as blank verse, and the sense of failure Melville felt after that novel's publication spurred him to renewed study of verse techniques. I find it puzzling that Hollander does not include "The March into Virginia," one of Melville's best lyrics; but there is enough here—including parts of the long poem, *Clarel*, and the late verses in which Melville returns to his seagoing years—to convince me of his interest as a poet. Other novelists of the century (like William Dean Howells, Sarah Orne Jewett, and Edith Wharton) do not prove half so interesting in verse. We also have the strange free-verse poems of Stephen Crane, who fought the Civil War in his mind long after Melville had done so.

The struggle these poets evince is simultaneously a struggle with the nation's history and with the nature of poetry itself. Edgar Allan Poe, our nightmare Ariel, gave us the most rarefied poetics we have ever had. Of his "Philosophy of Composition" Richard Wilbur has written: "There has never been a grander conception of poetry, nor a more impoverished one." Indeed Hollander's great anthology proves again and again the centrality of the marginal in American poetry. We have our masterpieces, but we also have our oddities— disturbing or amusing poems we preserve, or ought to preserve, for their singularity. Since Poe is commonly discussed in our time, I will devote my final paragraphs to relatively neglected writers.

I'm thinking not only of the songs of Katherine Lee Bates, Julia Ward Howe, and Stephen Foster, but of Eugene Field's poems for children, Ernest Lawrence Thayer's "Casey at the Bat," and Rose Terry Cooke's fine psychological poem called "Blue-Beard's Closet." I'm thinking of characters like the Ohioan Daniel Decatur Emmett who wrote "Dixie's Land," the unofficial anthem of the Confederacy, and recalling single poems of striking relevance (if not accomplishment) like Josiah D. Canning's "The Journalist." Hollander's inclusion of such works reminds us of the breadth of poetry's attraction and necessity in a utilitarian society.

Great men like John Quincy Adams and Abraham Lincoln wrote

verses, and in their time the meters of traditional verse were commonly known and cherished — a contrast to the prosaic poems of Jimmy Carter. Reviewing the Hollander anthology for the *TLS* (March 4, 1994), Hugh Kenner delighted in verses by our sixth President in which a clever rhyme was found for Pococatapetl — imagine Carter or most of our contemporaries pulling that one off! The spirit of play was not squelched in our relatively puritan country, but was everywhere in evidence, from Mark Twain to the felicitous Christopher Pearse Cranch, who called electricity "the soul of the nineteenth century." Cranch's "An Old Cat's Confessions" would have done Possum Eliot proud; his "Bird Language" is a sprightly precursor of Frost; and "Music" must have amused his audience when it was read at the annual dinner of the Harvard Musical Association in 1874. It begins:

> When "Music, Heavenly Maid," was very young,
> She did not sing as poets say she sung.
> Unlike the mermaids of the fairy tales,
> She paid but slight attention to her scales.

We also have Emma Lazarus, whose sonnet "The New Colossus" remains one of the best known pieces of public verse ever composed:

> Not like the brazen giant of Greek fame,
> With conquering limbs astride from land to land;
> Here at our sea-washed, sunset gates shall stand
> A mighty woman with a torch, whose flame
> Is the imprisoned lightning, and her name
> Mother of Exiles. From her beacon-hand
> Glows world-wide welcome; her mild eyes command
> The air-bridged harbor that twin cities frame.
> "Keep, ancient lands, your storied pomp!" cries she
> With silent lips. "Give me your tired, your poor,
> Your huddled masses yearning to breathe free,
> The wretched refuse of your teeming shore.
> Send these, the homeless, tempest-tost to me,
> I lift my lamp beside the golden door!"

Despite our violent family arguments about race, sex, immigration, and the economy, the United States remains a "golden" land to much of the world. Some of the patriotism on display in Hollander's anthology is hard for this baby-boomer to swallow, yet it conveys a truth about the hopes inherent in our origins and institutions.

How instructive it is, then, to turn to the verses of Ambrose Bierce, whose acid tongue came not only from his wretched upbringing (his view of farm life was brutally honest), but from his bitter combat experience. In many ways Bierce remains our truest Civil War writer. His satirical verses leave nothing sacred:

> Fiercely the battle raged and, sad to tell,
> Our corporal heroically fell!
> Fame from her height looked down upon the brawl
> And said, "He hadn't very far to fall."

He called his writing "fiddle-faddle in a minor key," but what a tart minor key it was, blessed with invective and mordant wit. His disappearance into revolutionary Mexico in 1913, and probable death at the Battle of Ojinaga in January 1914, leaves us one of our enduring literary mysteries, a story of America's dark side even more compelling than that of the vanished Weldon Kees.

One leaves Hollander's anthology conscious that "the national character" is a character in every sense of the word. Our stately mansions have stood side by side with the shanties of failures and ragamuffins, and our poets have survived or lost themselves in high and low society—and in every imaginable way. One learns from Hollander's notes that James Whitcomb Riley (author of some hilarious poems) once toured the Midwest with a medicine show, that Edwin Arlington Robinson worked briefly as a personal secretary to Harvard's president Charles W. Eliot, then moved on to obscurity in New York until his poems were championed by none other than President Theodore Roosevelt. One finds the good work of Trumbull Stickney, a brilliant classicist whose friends included George Cabot Lodge and Henry Adams, and who died of a brain tumor at the age of thirty. One is reminded of the popular poems of Edwin Markham, and introduced to relatively forgotten writers like Hamlin Garland, whose evocations of prairie life make simple, durable poems that repay rereading.

Too much of our heritage has been cast away; Hollander retrieves some of it for us at the close of another century. We have always been a nation of change and movement, always leaving much that we once valued beside the trail. Now our settlements thrive or decay in the shifting nature of our economy. As my wife and I drove on through Nebraska, we listened on public radio to another American poet, Ted Kooser, reading an essay about garage sales, those curious assemblies of treasure and detritus that teach us who we are by reminding us of what we have lost, what we ought to save.

ROBERT FROST, SEAMUS HEANEY, AND THE WELLSPRINGS OF POETRY

"What's that? Water. Ah, that's intelligent."
— Ernest Hemingway

The writers we discover for ourselves, unprompted by teachers or friends, often have a special place in our lives. They may or may not be writers of the first rank, but because we stumble onto them at an opportune moment they always stay with us. That only partly explains my long-standing affection for the work of Seamus Heaney—I knew about him before my professors did, and I was blissfully unaware that plenty of other readers had already made the same discovery. In college I used to haunt the library periodical stacks, and I recall reading an article about Heaney in a glossy, short-lived magazine called *Quest*. I walked downtown there in Colorado Springs and promptly ordered his new book, *North*. It was 1975. I had just returned to college from a year in which I made money by unloading crab boats in Alaska, then hitch-hiked for seven months through Britain and Ireland, including a few days in Belfast. Though I knew little of Irish literature and dimly comprehended Heaney's metaphorical use of the bogs, what attracted me to the poems was a whole verbal texture that seemed excitingly unfamiliar, and the whiff of something dangerously significant in their political subject matter. Here was a poet with a public.

Since that time I have followed Heaney's career with an almost proprietary interest. Though I now feel equal affection for the work of other contemporary poets, Derek Mahon among them, I continue to believe that Heaney is a brilliant literary figure. At this writing he is 58 years old; even without the Nobel Prize, he would still have made an impact on his times, and who knows what may yet lie ahead for him? It's still too early to pass final judgment on him or make the sort of sweeping proclamations, thumbs up or thumbs down, others have made, but it's not too early to confess the pleasure I take in his work, or to discern why it is that I like what I like in it.

In the past few years, I have had many conversations about Heaney with my friend John Devitt, a Dublin teacher and critic, and it was John who first gave me the idea for this essay, telling me of a spontaneous session in which he and Heaney had recited a great many Frost poems together. The anecdote fascinated me because Frost is my favorite American poet, and I am continually reminded of his popularity overseas. Then John pointed me to "Above the Brim," Heaney's excellent essay on Frost, in which one feels that the poet is defining himself, or part of himself, in relation to his subject.

For most readers, the differences between these two poets may be more obvious than any similarities. Heaney the Ulster Catholic farm boy turned academic, Frost of Scottish stock, the son of a Swedenborgian Christian and a journalist who had sympathized with the South in the American Civil War. Heaney was born to the farm, while Frost came to it relatively late. Heaney has found political subjects unavoidable, and has written of their painful complexity with both feeling and tact, while Frost maintained (in "The Figure a Poem Makes"), "Political freedom is nothing to me. I bestow it right and left." And of course Frost never would have countenanced Heaney's prosodic experiments or understood their partial debt to the Irish language tradition.

Yet, if I may compare them in the present tense, both are popular poets, no matter what the critics say about them. Both are learned teachers, yet both would agree with Wallace Stevens that "The greatest poverty is not to live/In a physical world." Both write well about manual labor and the mysteries of perception embodied in nature. These are issues I want to touch upon, but first I want to notice an even more particular matter of technique. Both Frost and Heaney have made use of colloquial speech in their poetry, refreshing rhythm and idiom with materials that are at least partly extra-literary.

Anyone who has ever tried to write verse knows that technical mastery is the price of admission, as it were, utterly necessary but also insufficient. One might say that too many poets have tried to "gain entry" without first earning the ticket, but one must also have ideas and a full-bodied sense of experience, not to mention the ability to tap one's own sources of urgency in the work. In "Above the Brim," Heaney refers to Frost's "artesian energies" (a phrase he used earlier to describe Kavanagh), as if poetry arose from underground springs—and of course it does. But once it arises, once the inspirational water surfaces, how is one to catch and hold it and allow others to drink from it? Clearly, the language of one's own time, the resources genuinely at one's own command, present the best opportunities. In the course of this essay, I will draw connections between seemingly disparate images—work, play, and water—to suggest that Frost and Heaney often adopt a similar stance toward poetic inspiration. That stance has much to do, of course, with their technique.

Discussing Frost's colloquial rhythms, Heaney quotes several familiar lyrics, including "Desert Places." Here is the first stanza of that poem:

> Snow falling and night falling fast, oh, fast
> In a field I looked into going past,
> And the ground almost covered smooth in snow,
> But a few weeds and stubble showing last.

And here is what Heaney says about it:

> The curves and grains of the first two lines of "Desert Places" are correspondingly native to living speech, without any tonal falsity. Who really notices that the letter "f" alliterates five times within thirteen syllables? It is no denigration of Hopkins to say that when such an alliterative cluster happens in his work, the reader is the first to notice it. With Frost, its effect is surely known, like a cold air that steals across a face; but until the lines are deliberately dwelt upon a moment like this, we do not even think of it as an "effect," and the means that produce it remain as unshowy as the grain in the wood.

Of course, to those who love lumber, the grain is quite noticeable, its whorls providing visual and tactile pleasures much like the poet's audible ones. Heaney is talking on one level about art that, following Horace's advice, disguises its artfulness; on another level he's talking about meter—not meter imposed upon speech, but meter propelled by and barely containing speech. It's the sort of balancing act that, in Heaney's terms, distinguishes genuine technique from mere craft. In his second stanza, Frost commits what to a purist might be unpardonable sins—using the pronoun "it" three times in one line, for example, yet his lines succeed:

The woods around it have it—it is theirs.
All animals are smothered in their lairs.
I am too absent-spirited to count;
The loneliness includes me unawares.

Frost's poem is tightly controlled yet colloquial, a masterpiece of its kind. Perhaps Heaney is thinking of such colloquial models when he creates some of his own effects, such as the voice of the fisherman in "Casualty," saying, "Puzzle me/The right answer to that one." In "Man and Boy," a poem from *Seeing Things*, Heaney moves back and forth between lofty diction and a kind of Frostian, deceptively casual line. Here is the second part of the poem:

In earshot of the pool where the salmon jumped
Back through its own unheard concentric soundwaves
A mower leans forever on his scythe.

He has mown himself to the center of the field
And stands in a final perfect ring
Of sunlit stubble.

'Go and tell your father,' the mower says
(He said it to my father who told me),
 'I have it mowed as clean as a new sixpence.'

My father is a barefoot boy with news,
Running at eye-level with weeds and stooks
On the afternoon of his own father's death.

The open, black half of the half-door waits.
I feel much heat and hurry in the air.
I feel his legs and quick heels far away

And strange as my own—when he will piggyback me
At a great height, light-headed and thin-boned,
Like a witless elder rescued from the fire.

Perhaps it is the casual use of parentheses here that reminds me of Frost, or the bits of quoted speech, or the precise description of

"The open, black half of the half-door...." There is also a Frostian slyness in the way he toys with an image from the *Aeneid* in his last stanza. Perhaps, too, it is the almost timeless image of the mower, calling to mind several of Frost's poems, but especially the sonnet "Mowing":

> There was never a sound beside the wood but one,
> And that was my long scythe whispering to the ground.
> What was it it whispered? I knew not well myself;
> Perhaps it was something about the heat of the sun,
> Something, perhaps, about the lack of sound—
> And that was why it whispered and did not speak.
> It was no dream of the gift of idle hours,
> Or easy gold at the hand of fay or elf:
> Anything more than the truth would have seemed too weak
> To the earnest love that laid the swale in rows,
> Not without feeble-pointed spikes of flowers
> (Pale orchises), and scared a bright green snake.
> The fact is the sweetest dream that labor knows.
> My long scythe whispered and left the hay to make.

When Frost writes about manual labor it is not to create a sentimental pastoral image; he is too tough-minded to be sentimental about rural life. He writes, I would say, out of the experience of work and the self-forgetfulness of work. It is what work has in common with play, touching on our strongest impressions of what it is to be alive in the world. In another context he would speak about work that is "play for mortal stakes," one of the best definitions of poetry I know, especially because it does not only define poetry. Existence for Frost is known through the body, yet something in it remains unknown. "What was it it whispered?" he asks in "Mowing," as if he would learn the language of the scythe and doubts that he can make it sing. "Anything more than the truth would have seemed too weak/To the earnest love that laid the swale in rows,/Not without feeble-pointed spikes of flowers/(Pale orchises), and scared a bright green snake." Frost allegorizes nature, puts the danger in his Eden—or is the snake harmless?—in order to challenge allegory itself: what do these things mean? "The fact is the sweetest dream that labor knows." Work and knowledge. Work as the act of knowing, or *The Work of Knowing,* as Richard Poirier aptly put it in the title of his excellent book on Frost. Whatever the scythe whispers, it leaves the hay to make, a bounty and *memento mori.*

Frost admired Emerson, and is often thought of in what might be called Emerson's neo-Platonic terms—that Emerson who said, "Nature is a symbol of spirit." Richard Wilbur sees Frost's message differently: "...our diminished age should not aspire to high visions and revelations; the thing to do is to keep faith with what has been revealed, and dwell in the shelter of it." But even Wilbur's interpretation allows for some degree of revelation, no matter how small. The fact may be only a dream because we do not know its ultimate relevance, but "the fact is the *sweetest* dream that labor knows." It can't be known without the motion of work, and I would say play as well. Here, perhaps, one assents to a truth one does not fully understand. "Let be be finale of seem," Wallace Stevens says, and Frost's mower swings that scythe somewhere between being and seeming.

In his essay on Frost, Heaney admires some of the qualities that can also be found in his own work. He refers to "a lifetime of pleasure in Frost's poems as events in language, flaunts and vaunts full of projective force and deliquescent backwash, the castings of a tide that lifts all spirits. Frost may have indeed declared that his whole anxiety was for himself as a performer, but the performance only succeeded fully when it launched itself beyond skill and ego into a run of energy that brimmed up outside the poet's conscious intention and control." This "play for mortal stakes" is a bit like that boy in Frost's "Birches" climbing toward heaven, only to have the thinning trunk bend and set him back upon the earth. Heaney has a similar image in "The Swing," a lovely, meditative sequence published in *The Spirit Level:*

> ...in the middle ground, the swing itself
> With an old lopsided sack in the loop of it,
> Perfectly still, hanging like pulley-slack,
> A lure let down to tempt the soul to rise.

He associates the playful suspension of swinging with something let down into a well, seeking those hidden waters and bringing them to the surface. Work and play join together, vocation and avocation, to use Frost's terms again, as if inspiration arose from such play for mortal stakes. They are important to the poet because they are central to human existence. They are not quite *what* we know but *how* we know.

As lovers of words, Frost and Heaney also love the motions and vocabularies associated with work and play. Heaney says he admires "the way [Frost] could describe (in 'The Code') how forkfuls of hay were built upon a wagonload for easy unloading later, when they have to be tossed down underfoot." Images of work occur from the beginning in Heaney's poems. The most obvious early examples are "Digging" and "Follower," both of which self-consciously reveal Heaney's distance from manual labor even as they vividly recall it: "The coarse boot nestled on the lug, the shaft/ Against the inside knee was levered firmly." The detail is precise, like that moment in Frost's great poem, "After Apple-Picking," when the speaker recalls exactly how the round rung of a ladder feels against his "instep arch." Both of these early Heaney poems are autobiographical, but both find parables of generational change in their descriptions of labor. Here is the whole text of "Follower":

> My father worked with a horse-plough,
> His shoulders globed like a full sail strung
> Between the shafts and the furrow.
> The horses strained at his clicking tongue.
>
> An expert. He would set the wing
> And fit the bright steel-pointed sock.
> The sod rolled over without breaking.
> And the headrig, with a single pluck
>
> Of reins, the sweating team turned round
> And back into the land. His eye
> Narrowed and angled at the ground,
> Mapping the furrow exactly.
>
> I stumbled in his hobnailed wake,
> Fell sometimes on the polished sod;
> Sometimes he rode me on his back
> Dipping and rising to his plod.

I wanted to grow up and plough,
To close one eye, stiffen my arm.
All I ever did was follow
In his broad shadow round the farm.

I was a nuisance, tripping, falling,
Yapping always. But today
It is my father who keeps stumbling
Behind me, and will not go away.

The technique of pararhyme common to many Heaney poems—plough/follow—has its roots in the Irish tradition, as Bernard O'Donoghue demonstrates in his book, *Seamus Heaney and the Language of Poetry.* Recently Heaney has more comfortably adopted traditional English accentual-syllabic meter, occasionally with full rhymes. But from early on he was adept at capturing the sounds and rhythms of certain kinds of work. His new book, *The Spirit Level,* which takes its title from a carpenter's tool, is also full of such passages, like this playful description of a mason at work:

Over and over, the slur, the scrape and mix
As he trowelled and retrowelled and laid down
Courses of glum mortar. Then the bricks
Jiggled and settled, tocked and tapped in line.

His gift for onomatopoeia, for matching sound and sense, is quite astonishing.

What I hope I have demonstrated here, and what Heaney freely admits, is that Frost is a touchstone poet for him; the American poet's technique and stance translates usefully to Ireland, to some of Heaney's own concerns as an artist. The association of poetry with other kinds of work and play is extremely helpful, a way of keeping poetry human, like the use of colloquialism with other kinds of diction and syntax.

In a poem called "The Backward Look" from *Wintering Out,* Heaney describes the movement of a snipe as follows:

A stagger in air
as if a language
failed, a sleight
of wing.

I happen to dislike the blatant comparison of that strange bird to something in language, or at least wish it had been more subtle, but that phrase, "sleight/of wing," has Frost's magician's touch — perhaps because it is a quotation of Frost's poem "Come In":

> As I came to the edge of the woods,
> Thrush music—hark!
> Now if it was dusk outside,
> Inside it was dark.
>
> Too dark in the woods for a bird
> By sleight of wing
> To better its perch for the night,
> Though it still could sing.
>
> The last of the light of the sun
> That had died in the west
> Still lived for one song more
> In a thrush's breast.
>
> Far in the pillared dark
> Thrush music went—
> Almost like a call to come in
> To the dark and lament.
>
> But no, I was out for stars:
> I would not come in.
> I meant not even if asked,
> And I hadn't been.

Like Heaney, Frost locates himself in a world that is hard to know, where one survives by work, cunning and wit. Heaney has rarely worked in such resolute meter and rhyme (techniques too many of our contemporaries mistrust). The traditional English meter of his fine early poem, "Requiem for the Croppies," seems to be coming back to him in the latter half of his career, beginning with "Casualty" in *Field Work*, and he has recently done a fine trochaic elegy for Joseph Brodsky.

Frost also has a metaphor that has not been quite so available to Heaney: the Dantesque forest in which we are trying to find our way. In both poetry and fairy tales, the path through the woods is associated with fundamental anxieties and resolutions. Perhaps we can only make small bits of order, like Frost's wood pile, in what we perceive to be a chaotic universe, or perhaps we can cultivate a garden there, or we can play a game, first marking off a football pitch, then setting rules, or we can climb a birch or swing suspended between heaven and earth. Knowledge and survival come together in such pleasureful activities, yet we intuit something beyond our knowledge—perhaps it is the goal of science or the solace of religion. Our experience may often be fragmentary, yet we may also believe that reality is not fragmented, a wholeness just beyond our ken. One apparently universal image of this principle is water, flowing and flown, changing and stable, clear and sustaining. "Thousands have lived without love," Auden reminds us, "not one without water." Water beats time on our shores, covers two-thirds of the earth, composes the largest part of our own bodies. Think of its magical properties. Water is a liquid that contains solids and very easily evaporates, becoming a gas. It is elemental, the source of life, associated with gods and the inspiration of poets. In *Phaedrus*, Socrates speaks on a summer's day in the shade of a plane tree beside a stream, and this veteran city-dweller claims to derive his inspiration, as he discourses on love and language, from the genius of that place.

Perhaps the poetic Muse is an antiquated notion, but the impulse to muse upon inspiration's sources is certainly not. Milton calls upon the "sisters of the sacred well/That from beneath the seat of Jove doth spring," and "Lycidas" becomes a veritable catalogue of waters bringing both death and resurrection. Michael Drayton refers to Ben Jonson, "Who had drunk deep of the Pierian spring." That spring was originally associated with Muse worship in the north of Greece, which eventually spread south toward Delphi and Mount Helicon, and I suppose it is also associated with the spring created by the winged horse Pegasus at Corinth. The sacred well of the Muses and of Pegasus was certainly in Frost's mind when he wrote "For Once, Then, Something," but the trickster in him won't grant the symbol an easy stability:

> Others taunt me with having knelt at well-curbs
> Always wrong to the light, so never seeing
> Deeper down in the well than where the water

Gives me back in a shining surface picture
Me myself in the summer heaven godlike
Looking out of a wreath of fern and cloud puffs.
Once, when trying with chin against a well-curb,
I discerned, as I thought, beyond the picture,
Through the picture, a something white, uncertain,
Something more of the depths—and then I lost it.
Water came to rebuke the too clear water.
One drop fell from a fern, and lo, a ripple
Shook whatever it was lay there at bottom,
Blurred it, blotted it out. What was that whiteness?
Truth? A pebble of quartz? For once, then, something.

As many other critics have noted, Frost tricks us into assigning meaning to his allegorical images. Is truth the whiteness seen at the bottom of a symbolic well? Some pollywog version of Moby Dick, perhaps? I sense him laughing here, depicting himself as his critics see him: a woodsy, narcissistic poet gazing down at his own image and finding a laureate's wreath in his reflection. But Frost's laughter is also serious. What is it we see when we look and when we assign our meanings? As in Auden's great poem "Atlantis," where the traveler never reaches the desired destination but is lucky even to glimpse it in a vision, Frost taunts his would-be tormentors by suggesting that his troubled sight may prove truer than their certainty. Part of this scoffing at his critics occurs in the very form he has chosen, classical hendecasyllabics, which, he says in a 1920 letter to G.R. Elliott, were "calculated to tease the metrists." Anyone who thinks Frost unsophisticated or undesigning is a damned fool.

Heaney's poetry can be said to begin with elemental earth and water, not only those amniotic bogs but also classical and modern wells. It's no accident that his early poem called "Personal Helicon" is dedicated to the classically trained poet Michael Longley:

As a child, they could not keep me from wells
And old pumps with buckets and windlasses.
I loved the dark drop, the trapped sky, the smells
Of waterweed, fungus and dark moss.

One, in a brickyard, with a rotted board top.
I savoured the rich crash when a bucket
Plummeted down at the end of a rope.
So deep you saw no reflection in it.

A shallow one under a dry stone ditch
Fructified like any aquarium.
When you dragged out long roots from the soft mulch
A white face hovered over the bottom.

Others had echoes, gave back your own call
With a clean new music in it. And one
Was scaresome, for there, out of ferns and tall
Foxgloves, a rat slapped across my reflection.

Now, to pry into roots, to finger slime,
To stare, big-eyed Narcissus, into some spring
Is beneath all adult dignity. I rhyme
To see myself, to set the darkness echoing.

I cannot imagine Heaney writing this poem without recalling Frost.
Though he personalizes the images, he plays with the same charge
of childish narcissism that is so often leveled against poets. He even
accepts it: "I rhyme/To see myself...." But, like Frost, he assumes a
deeper mystery in the well even as he questions it; he also rhymes
"to set the darkness echoing." The disembodied voice of that echo
may lie at the heart of poetry's anxious triumph. What does it all
mean? What good is it? What does it have to do with life as we live
it, the world's heartbreaking beauty and trouble?

Both Heaney and Frost answer such questions with sly games
and parables. They remind us that what is sacred can also be terri-
fying. In "Once by the Pacific" Frost recalls the territory where he
was born, at the western extreme of American expansion, where
the vast ocean seems an image of the destructive element:

The shattered water made a misty din.
Great waves looked over others coming in,
And thought of doing something to the shore
That water never did to land before.

The clouds were low and hairy in the skies,
Like locks blown forward in the gleam of eyes.
You could not tell, and yet it looked as if
The shore was lucky in being backed by cliff,
The cliff in being backed by continent;
It looked as if a night of dark intent
Was coming, and not only a night, an age.
Someone had better be prepared for rage.
There would be more than ocean-water broken
Before God's last *Put out the light* was spoken.

Come to think of it, there's something amniotic in the breaking water here as well, though the italicized quotation of murderous, irrational Othello—*Put out the light*—is almost the last word. I recall an Andrei Konchalavsky film called *Runaway Train*, based on a story by Akira Kurosawa, in which Jon Voight portrays a killer escaping from a prison somewhere in the frozen wasteland of a symbolic Alaska. Voight's character is a defiant force, ultimately inexplicable, the sort of thing the Greeks comprehended in their portrayals of Dionysus. Frost faces a similar blind force in his poem.

The irrational element in Heaney's poetry derives at least partly from the political situation of his homeland, the sheer brutality of an argument based upon prejudice and blind pride, and Heaney's responses to this predicament have been both shrewd and responsible. Some of his strongest poems about such violence are in the latest book, poems like "Keeping Going" and "Mycenae Lookout," in which he seems to see the violence as a timeless human impulse. While acknowledging the precariousness of his position, Heaney has consistently refused to speak for a group or tribe. Like Frost, he insists upon the freedom of the poet to make his own way in the world, distinct from the madness of crowds.

I must confess that I do not yet fully understand the visionary aspects of his last two books, *Seeing Things* and *The Spirit Level*. He seems to be taking a great risk, perhaps partly letting go of the skepticism one often finds in Frost. In one sense, Heaney's self-consciousness about language keeps him at a remove from life, so his visionary leaps seem wishful thinking more than accomplished experiences. What I can say is that images of work, play and water pervade these poems. In "The Rain Stick," which opens the new collection, one even finds some of the same vocabulary used in Heaney's descriptions of Frost:

> Upend the rain stick and what happens next
> Is a music that you never could have known
> To listen for. In a cactus stalk
>
> Downpour, sluice-rush, spillage and backwash
> Come flowing through. You stand there like a pipe
> Being played by water, you shake it again lightly
>
> And diminuendo runs through all its scales
> Like a gutter stopping trickling. And now here comes
> A sprinkle of drops out of the freshened leaves,
>
> Then subtle little wets off grass and daisies;
> The glitter-drizzle, almost-breath of air.
> Upend the stick again. What happens next
>
> Is undiminished for having happened once,
> Twice, ten, a thousand times before.
> Who cares if all the music that transpires
>
> Is the fall of grit or dry seeds through a cactus?
> You are like a rich man entering heaven
> Through the ear of a raindrop. Listen now again.

It is not rain that Heaney hears, but an approximation of rain. Does this mean that the poet who called his Nobel lecture "Crediting Poetry" has trouble really crediting poetry himself? Is language always a barrier between us and experience, and is this why Heaney has sometimes avoided resolute form in his work? It seems to me that the experience of Heaney's poems is a mixture of directness and indirectness, and that this stance presents both dangers and human pleasures. Play becomes essential, like the contrary "spirit" of Frost's "West-Running Brook":

> "It is this backward motion toward the source,
> Against the stream, that most we see ourselves in,

The tribute of the current to the source.
It is from this in nature we are from.
It is most us."

Whatever the sources of the poetic imagination, Heaney seems to have learned as much about them from Frost as from his more commonly acknowledged non-Irish masters, Dante, Mandelstam and Lowell. Dante's allegory underlies Frost's as well, yet Frost makes it uniquely his own. His *Collected Poems* contains some work that I would not want to save, but the best of it conveys an indomitable spirit, in form if not in content. Heaney describes the man and the work well:

> Demonically intelligent, as acute about his own masquerades as he was about others', Frost obeyed the ancient command to know himself. Like Yeats at the end of "Dialogue of Self and Soul," Frost would be "content to live it all again," and be content also to "cast out remorse." Unlike Yeats, however, he would expect neither a flow of sweetness into his breast nor a flash of beatitude upon the world to ensue from any such bout of self-exculpation. He made no secret of the prejudice and contrariness at the centre of his nature, and never shirked the bleakness of that last place in himself.

All of that is true, but Frost also knows how to laugh at himself, and perhaps it is some of that canny humor that Heaney has now discovered for himself.

In his famous, relatively late poem called "Directive" (which Heaney quotes in *The Redress of Poetry*), Frost Americanizes the sacred spring as well as the Arthurian quest for the Grail. His traveler, by implication his reader, seeks the sustaining water, the Grail, in a landscape of natural change as vast as the last glacier, as quick and skittish as the animals now inhabiting the woods. These woods seem to have overgrown a farm or homestead, as well as a smaller house where children once played. "Weep for what little things could make them glad," he says. He presents himself as a kind of Virgil, a poet guide, but in this case a guide "Who only has at heart your getting lost." I suppose this landscape is purgatorial, somewhere between hell and paradise, partly mitigated by the questing spirit. Frost views life as a struggle, but he understands that the human spirit does not survive only by practical means. One cannot find the poet's hidden grail unless one learns to accept the fact of being lost, and to play in spite of it — perhaps I should say to play *because* of it. "Here are your waters and your watering place," Frost says at last. "Drink and be whole again beyond confusion."

IRISH POETRY AT THE CROSSROADS

When I was born the row began...
—Louis MacNeice

I have a friend whom I think of as the quintessential Dubliner, a veritable volcano of intellectual energies, his mind fired by deep sympathies and vast learning that make him one of the most incandescent conversationalists I have ever met.[1] In the summer of 1996 I had the good fortune to spend a few days with him in Dublin and its environs, places he knows with an intimate historical sense foreign to most Americans. Incapable of dullness, he could talk about almost anything. One moment he surveyed the settings of stories by Joyce or Beckett, the next he cherished the intricacies of cricket, nodding politely at my comparisons to baseball. He recited a massively sinuous sentence by Milton to illustrate verbal athleticism of a related kind, marked how Yeats had learned from such syntax, then darted into the poetry of Virgil, followed by current Irish politics, where he dismissed one government minister with vernacular brio: "The man's as t'ick as two planks!"

America, I sometimes feel, douses its own intellectual fires. Our country is so large, so various, that it both exhilarates and wears us out. I tried conveying this dilemma to my friend, contrasting American to Irish society, where it seems that everyone knows everyone else. Though the Irish may be a private people, they have no anonymity. My friend, of course, responded with an anecdote. We were driving along a residential street, and he told me he had once seen Seamus Heaney strolling along the same avenue and pulled over for a chat. At the time he had French guests with him in the car, and when he eased back into traffic they inquired about the amiable man to whom he had been talking. "Oh that fella?" my friend told them. "That's the fucker who's going to win the Nobel Prize." He leaned toward me with an expression of delight, transforming the word "fucker" to a proud and affectionate superlative.

Dare I say that the range and passion of my friend's conversation is particularly Irish? It seems that Irish writers and intellectuals live in a pressure-cooker of linguistic and social strategizing. This can be exhausting—I would never blame an Irish writer for wanting out of the fray—but also quite intoxicating. In his superb, beautifully-written collection of literary essays, *The Pressed Melodeon*, the American poet Ben Howard muses upon the attractiveness of Ireland and its writers to the rest of us. This is a book forged by long experience with Ireland, deep learning about poetry and a talent for exacting observation. Toward the end of his title essay, he writes that

> it is heartening to visit an English-speaking country where the idea of the poet is still taken seriously. Irish writers complain that their culture pays lip service to Poetry while neglecting poets and letting national treasures like Coole Park fall into ruin. Their point is well taken, but it is pleasing, nonetheless, to visit a country where poems are reproduced in holograph on village monuments, where the faces of poets—Swift, Yeats—appear on the currency, where full-time writers are exempt from income tax and where poets like Kavanagh are remembered so passionately, both by poets and lay people.

I would add that it is deeply refreshing to see politics, history, sport and literature discussed side by side in the letters columns of *The Irish Times* and other papers, and to see poetry discussed in the major media instead of marginalized, as it often is in the United States—just look for poetry reviews in the increasingly vapid *New York Times Book Review* and you'll see what I mean.

We Americans who love Irish poetry do so in part, I think, because we find in it qualities missing from too much of our own: verbal rigor wedded to a strong, if conflicted, social sense, poets who write as if writing mattered. Of course I overgeneralize, but I think Ben Howard is right about Ireland when he discusses "the power of language in a country so politicized, so keenly aware of nuances and innuendoes." I can't gauge the degree to which we sentimentalize Ireland when we think in these terms, yet Irish writers have made similar observations.

None of this would matter if Irish writers hadn't written particularly well. But they have. Think of the four Nobel Prizewinners—Yeats, Shaw, Beckett and Heaney—then add Joyce, Flann O'Brien, Frank O'Conner, Patrick Kavanagh, Louis MacNeice and dozens of others. Of course there are dissenting voices, those who would note the all-male list I have just given. Eileen Battersby, an

American living in Ireland, observes the injustices of "Ireland's conservative political tradition," and the poet-critic Peter Sirr has identified a similar conservatism in contemporary Irish poetry: "It tends to avoid formal experiment, jealously hoards its clarities, its logic, its trove of paraphrasable content." I confess I have trouble understanding why that's such an awful state of affairs, but I fully understand the perception among women and younger writers that an essentially conservative male cadre dominates Irish literature. In *The Living Stream*, the Belfast critic Edna Longley describes an alternative "aesthetic revisionism": "...the formal order established by Heaney, [Michael] Longley and Mahon has been challenged by the equally concentrated but more open-ended methods of Muldoon, Ciaran Carson and Medbh McGuckian." This seems historically accurate; there is a kind of ferment in contemporary Irish literature, but the taste of these younger writers is more academic than avant-garde. Furthermore, as in America, too few critics engage in the difficult task of trying to enunciate aesthetic standards, asking what makes writing good or bad. One poet-critic, Dennis O'Driscoll, even comments on the impossibility of honest reviewing in a country where all the writers know each other.

However we define poetry, it lives, as it has always lived, at a crossroads between tradition and modernity, between notions of eternal truth and change. And however skeptical they may be about themselves, their art or their language, poets are usually in this business for the long haul. A poet may be afraid to believe in eternity, yet write as if the ages mattered, as if poetry were intended to cross time and whisper its intimacies to the ears of strangers. There are many good reasons for thinking that notions of permanence are mad, but great art demands them nonetheless. Ireland's place as an emerging nation, with its youthful energies, its ancient traditions, its Troubles and its grudging embrace of the English language, has given its poets admirable powers. But the crossroads implies choices, and in the following pages I will both question and applaud choices these poets have made.

Where to begin? The influence of Yeats on subsequent poets is stronger than their attempts to deny it, and *The Pressed Melodeon* contains fine essays on two other influential figures, MacNeice and Kavanagh. Howard takes his title, though, from a writer who is still very much alive. "To the sorrows of modern Ireland," he writes, "John Montague has brought an historian's understanding and a harper's delicate music. He has kept faith with his lyric gift while bearing witness to violent events." In this sense, Montague is a pivotal figure in contemporary Irish poetry. Wake Forest University Press, which performs a real service by making many Irish poets available in the States, has now brought out Montague's *Collected Poems*, a handsome volume in which we can see much justice in Howard's praise.

Montague's most influential book remains *The Rough Field* (1972), a collage of lyrics, reminiscences, historical fragments and meditations, which he later followed with another book-length sequence, *The Dead kingdom* (1984). In these books and others, Montague writes of a personal past containing elements of Irish national epic: emigration, poverty, his tough republican father, abandonment by his mother, life in America and on both sides of the Irish border. Ben Howard argues that Montague

> has told the story of Northern Ireland as no other poet has, tracing the present sectarian violence to its roots in Jacobean Ulster. Wary of the "lyric memory" that would "soften the fact" ("Dance Hall"), he has sought "exactness," employing a "low-pitched style" that will not "betray the event." Yet his quiet music has persisted, braced and chastened by its encounters with civil strife.

Given the breadth of this evolving program, it is no disgrace that Montague does not always succeed. I don't think his experiments with free verse, so clearly influenced by William Carlos Williams, always benefit his poems. For example, here are four stanzas from "Omagh Hospital":

> Your white hair
> on the thin rack
> of your shoulders
>
> it is hard to
> look into the eyes
> of the dying

who carry away
a part of oneself—
a shared world

& you, whose life
was selflessness
now die slowly

Williams' best poems are charged by surprising line breaks and pungent, active verbs, but here the "low-pitched style" intended not to "betray the event" seems relatively arbitrary. Call it a weakness, but I say a poet's lines ought to matter as lines a good percentage of the time. This becomes even more problematic for me in *The Dead kingdom*, nearly the whole book composed in the same narrow columns, some of which could easily be prose. Of course poets perennially argue in this way: how much to weight tradition, how much modernity. My point is simply that a poet's most distinctive resource is the line — everything else can be done in prose — so the medium of the line ought to be used to advantage.

Montague knows what he is doing, and my attention flags only when I read him at length. He has written poems that seem triumphant or nearly so, including "Like Dolmens Round My Childhood...," "Herbert Street Revisited," "A Flowering Absence," "The Locket," "Red Branch," 'The Water Carrier," A Drink of Milk" and "The Trout." One of his strengths is for capturing characters in verse, as he does in "Clear the Way":

Her only revenge on her hasty lovers
Was to call each child after its father,
Which the locals admired, and seeing her saunter
To collect the pension of her soldier husband
Trailed by her army of baby Irregulars.

Using the loaded word "Irregulars" as a stand-in for "bastards" shows real confidence in his audience.

Montague has also been willing to challenge the conservatism of Irish culture by the frankness with which he writes about love and sex: "As my Province burns/I sing of love,/ Hoping to give that fiery/Wheel a shove." Here is his poem to the Celtic earth goddess often depicted on Irish churches, "Sheela Na Gig":

> The bloody tent-flap opens. We slide
> into life, slick with slime and blood.
> Cunt or Cymric *cwm*, Chaucerian *quente*,
> the first home from which man is sent
> into banishment, to spend his whole life
> cruising to return, raising a puny mast
> to sail back into those moist lips
> that overhang *labia minora* and *clitoris*.
> To sigh and die upon the Mount of Venus,
> layer after layer of warm moss,
> to return to that first darkness!
> Small wonder she grins at us, from gable
> or church wall. For the howling babe
> life's warm start: man's question mark.

Ultimately, re-reading Montague's work, I find a breadth that some-times sacrifices the heights of poetry to capture private and public histories; his *Collected Poems* is terribly important to any understand-ing of Irish poetry at the perpetual crossroads of tradition and modernity.

The contemporary Irish poet I like best is Derek Mahon, some of whose lyrics I find literally unforgettable. Perhaps he doesn't have the breadth of Montague or the warmth of Heaney, but as Ben Howard convincingly argues, Mahon raises irony to a level "of prophetic vision." He has long been a formal master, as one can see in poems like "In Carrodore Churchyard," "The Terminal Bar," "Afterlives," "Everything is Going to Be All Right" and "Dawn at St. Patricks." Other critics note the humanizing ironies of poems like "The Mute Phenomena," "A Disused Shed in Co. Wexford," "Lives" and "The Snow Party." Throughout much of his work Mahon seems, like Louis MacNeice, an uncomfortable Irishman, often writing from abroad with a cosmopolitan sense of the world. In his review of *The Hunt By Night*, Ben Howard begins, "Exile is the birthright of the Irish poet," then brilliantly demonstrates that such exile is not only geographical but psychological as well, the poet holding himself at bay.

Recently Mahon has dared to be more personal and direct; I don't think it has harmed him. His new book, *The Hudson Letter*, shows him at work in a more loose-limbed manner, but the level of his achievement remains extremely high. *The Hudson Letter* is really two books, the first published by Gallery Press in Ireland, the second, revised edition by Wake Forest. I regret only one change Mahon has made, dropping "The Yaddo Letter" from the American edition, probably because it is also available in one version of his recent *Selected Poems*. Otherwise, it seems to me that, by removing some weaker poems, he has greatly clarified the intellectual lineaments of the collection.

The title sequence comprises eighteen poems that range over life in New York (where Mahon has taught at NYU), thoughts on women and feminism arising in the aftermath of divorce, and the lives of other "exiles" in New York like W.H. Auden and J.B. Yeats. Occasionally in heroic couplets, the poems never stray far from pentameter, though Mahon's meters are sometimes quite free. His range of diction, derived from street slang, TV, popular music, newspapers, opera, classical and modern authors, is wonderfully unpredictable, as if Mahon had simply given himself permission to have fun with the epistolary tradition. But the sequence is also subtly guided by its themes. Here the poet addresses one of his children:

> ...and yet, across 3,000 miles of water
> and five time zones, my own prayer for my daughter
> would be, not innocence and ceremony
> exactly, but a more complicated grace,
> the sort of thing you play on the boxed lyre when you're alone
> in the House of Atreus, something slow and meditative,
> some rich myth of reconciliation
> as if a statue moved and began to live—
> for I like to think all this is a winter's tale
> around a hearth (but whose?); and that when we tell
> the story ten years hence you'll be able to say,
> 'Thou mettest with things dying, I with things new-born.'

That moving statue alludes not only to Shakespeare and reconciliation; it also suggests Ovid's version of Pygmalion and Galatea, with all its ambiguities about creation and desire. Mahon's beautiful translation of the Ovid passage is, in fact, the second poem in the present collection. The first is "Noon at St. Michael's," detailing a relationship with a real woman who has apparently reminded the poet just how real she is. *The Hudson Letter* appears to be partly a book about facing women—ex-wife, lover, daughter—as real beings rather than as symbols. The one translation from the Irish he includes is a poem by Nuala Ni Dhomhnaill, justly celebrated for her sensuality, but in this case a poem about rejection: "Outside/the warm conspiracy of your love/I stand, a nobody,/an orphan at the door."

Ovid and Shakespeare, exile, desire and reconciliation—these were contained in the address to his daughter I quoted, but he also imagined a song in the House of Atreus, a place of slaughter and a source of tragedy. When he later writes, "The reed-voiced nightingale has been my guide," Mahon adopts the voice of Sappho: "Nothing was alien to me, nothing inhuman:/ what did I teach but the love of women?" He follows that section with another called "Beauty and the Beast," dedicated to Fay Wray. Perhaps some of this is explained in the section on J.B. Yeats: "Thus your epiphany, and you wrote to explain:/ 'The nightingale sings with its breast against a thorn,/ it's out of pain that personality is born'...." But Mahon won't leave it at that; he follows the romantic nightingale with the more comical yellow bittern, famous in Irish poetry for having died from lack of drink. With its varied meditations on love, beauty and responsibility, *The Hudson Letter* is a magnificently playful book, intricately designed and executed, a worthy addition to the Mahon canon.

For a time, Mahon's roommate at Trinity College was another Belfast poet, Michael Longley, whose work has received far less attention than that of Mahon and Heaney. Reading through Longley's earlier *Selected Poems*, it does seem that he has taken longer to write poems that are distinctly his own. With *Gorse Fires* and, now, *The Ghost Orchid*, Longley has established his reputation. It's striking just how much of his best work derives from translation, particularly of Homer and Ovid. This is a genially learned poet who has stayed on in Belfast through the Troubles—and even survived a career as an arts administrator. There's something both precise and unpretentious in his work, a kind of monument to civility and love in a brutalized society. In the new book I especially like the playfulness of "The Mad Poet," the gravity of "Ivory & Water" and "Baucis and Philemon." But, like it or not, *The Ghost Orchid* will always be known as the book in which Longley published "Ceasefire."

Few Americans can know the impact this one sonnet has had since its publication, by lucky accident, in *The Irish Times* the day after the IRA announced its ceasefire in 1994. In the weeks before, the Troubles had been particularly bloody, so the new negotiations gave Ireland its most hopeful reprieve in a generation. At the time too few people realized that Longley's poem perfectly expressed the dilemma a ceasefire would present; in its euphoria over peace, the general population would try to forget the very real wounds and griefs of those who had actually lost family in the struggle. The woundedness and hatred would not just disappear, but would underlie any reconciliation, waiting to be acknowledged. Here is Longley's superb poem (borrowing from Homer):

I.

Put in mind of his own father and moved to tears
Achilles took him by the hand and pushed the old king
Gently away, but Priam curled up at his feet and
Wept with him until their sadness filled the building.

II.

Taking Hector's corpse into his own hands Achilles
Made sure it was washed and, for the old king's sake,
Laid out in uniform, ready for Priam to carry
Wrapped like a present home to Troy at daybreak.

III.

When they had eaten together, It pleased them both
To stare at each other's beauty as lovers might,
Achilles built like a god, Priam good-looking still
And full of conversation, who earlier had sighed:

IV.

'I get down on my knees and do what must be done
And kiss Achilles' hand, the killer of my son.'

The bitterness of reconciliation in the poem's final couplet is the last thing we encounter, yet Priam made this statement at a moment before the rest of the poem takes place. Longley's rearrangement of chronology leaves us with the grief we had hoped would wither away. All the conflicted feelings are there, memorably expressed, and I have no reservations whatsoever is saying that "Ceasefire" is one of the most important poems of Longley's generation.

The fact that some of his best work (and some of Mahon's) derives from translation leads me to the curious case of Nuala Ni Dhomhnaill; I want to call her a fine poet, but I cannot read her in the original Irish. I never know whether what delights me in her work is attributable to her or to the many poets who have translated her. From interviews and articles about her, I have the sense of a highly intelligent, articulate and worldly person whose commitment to Irish is truly a poetic one, born of a passion for the language. Beyond that, I'm in her translators' considerable debt.

And she has been lucky. *Pharaoh's Daughter* contains poems translated by Seamus Heaney, Derek Mahon, Paul Muldoon, Michael Hartnett, Medbh McGuckian, John Montague—in short, by the cream of the Irish poetry establishment. Along with other poets like Gabriel Rosenstock, Ni Dhomhnaill has made it her business to modernize the Irish tongue; in doing so, she preserves and reformulates a rich historical and mythological heritage. But she does this without seeming exclusively local. I can't prove it, but I sense that—by writing in Irish and working with translators—Ni Dhomhnaill makes things accessible to us that we wouldn't encounter by other means. One example of good work in *Pharaoh's Daughter* is "Aubade," translated by Michael Longley:

> It's all the same to morning what it dawns on—
> On the bickering of jackdaws in leafy trees;
> On that dandy from the wetlands, the green mallard's
> Stylish glissando among reeds; on the moorhen
> Whose white petticoat flickers around the boghole;
> On the oystercatcher on tiptoe at low tide.
>
> It's all the same to the sun what it rises on—
> On the windows in houses in Georgian squares;

On bees swarming to blitz suburban gardens;
On young couples yawning in unison before
They do it again; on dew like sweat or tears
On lilies and roses; on your bare shoulders.

But it isn't all the same to us that night-time
Runs out; that we must make do with today's
Happenings, and stoop and somehow glue together
The silly little shards of our lives, so that
Our children can drink water from broken bowls,
Not cupped hands. It isn't the same at all.

Wake Forest has also published Ni Dhomhnaill's new collection, *The Astrakhan Cloak*, translated by the erratically talented Paul Muldoon. Once again the best poems seem fresh and natural, as good translations should: "There's a crack In the flight of stairs/ at my very core/that I simply can't get round or traverse." Like Muldoon himself, Ni Dhomhnaill can enjoy dissing an old myth. Just compare Yeats' early versions of Mother Ireland to Ni Dhomhnaill's "Cathleen":

You can't take her out for a night on the town
without her either showing you up or badly letting you down:
just because she made the Twenties roar
with her Black and Tan bottom—O Terpsichore—
and her hair in a permanent wave....

The mention of Cathleen reminds me that the Irish language is not the only context in which Ni Dhomhnaill's poems have been discussed. There is also the issue of feminism in a country that has been famously backward concerning women's rights. Among women poets, Eavan Boland has made the loudest noise about the difficulties she has faced, and now that she has her American professorship (at Stanford), one would hope she would feel confident enough to concentrate on writing stronger poems. The truth is, there are several very good poets in Ireland—Paula Meehan and Mary O'Malley spring to mind, among others—who seem sure enough of themselves to write as women without self-aggrandizing political pronouncements (though Boland should be credited for clearing a space for them). Insofar as I can judge, Ni Dhomhnaill seems part of their company. Some of her poems go on longer than necessary, risking shapelessness, but the best of them suggest that the subheading "Irish Women Poets" might legitimately be retired.

I'm less confident about Medbh McGuckian, who seems to enjoy being compared to Emily Dickinson (it's the most cryptic Dickinson and the undervalued woman who are symbolically important here). I've criticized McGuckian before, and I should confess that her new book, *Captain Lavender*, seems more accessible than her last. Frankly, my dislike of her work is less important than her defenses against such objections and what they imply about the state of poetry. I look for accuracy in poetry, memorable speech, something so well or beautifully said that it lifts me to another state of consciousness, but I have difficulty with poems that present unnecessary barriers to my comprehension. The new book contains cases in point, like "The Over Mother":

> In the sealed hotel men are handled
> as if they were furniture, and passion
> exhausts itself at the mouth. Play kisses
> stir the circuits of the underloved body
> to an ever-resurrection, a never-had tenderness
> that dies inside me.
>
> My cleverly dead and vertical audience,
> words fly out from your climate of unexpectation
> in leaky, shallowised night letters—
> what you has spoken?
>
> I keep seeing birds
> that could be you when you stretch out
> like a syllable and look to me
> as if I could give you wings

I'm not sure I can think of a better example of sheer pretentiousness in contemporary poetry. Are we really supposed to guess what "the sealed hotel" means, what kind of "passion/ exhausts itself at the mouth," or what "the underloved body" refers to? Are her critics the "cleverly dead and vertical ones" she apparently insults? Why the stretching out "like a syllable" instead of like something else? And if she can't give us wings, even momentary and imaginary ones, why in hell would we want her poetry? What is it for?

Ironically, it's Ni Dhomhnaill who supplies a kind of answer to my questions. She and McGuckian were jointly interviewed in *The Southern Review* (Summer 1995), where Ni Dhomhnaill refers to "the hysteria of what passes for literary criticism in the case of Medbh and me. Our *logos* is based on women's experience, on our lives, rather than on Platonic discourse." So readers like me are charged with upholding a defunct Platonic ideal of poetry; it's the perfect intellectual armor for McGuckian to hide behind, and it doesn't explain why I like McGuckian's translations of Ni Dhomhnaill better than McGuckian's own poems. When critics like Edna Longley praise her for her "teasing subversions, her dismantling of hierarchy and authority," my answer is stubbornly simple: why can't she make it all more fun to read? If "she writes a symbolic meta-language with its own emblematic grammar," well, pardon me for choosing to read someone else.

Mind you, I don't believe such literary fights can be easily settled; I'll move on from this one by quoting a stanza from Eilean Ni Chuilleanain's book, *The Brazen Serpent*. It's from a poem called "The Real Thing," partly about an illuminated manuscript:

> Her history is a blank sheet,
> Her vows a folded paper locked like a well.
> The torn end of the serpent
> Tilts the lace edge of the veil.
> The real thing, the one free foot kicking
> Under the white sheet of history.

Ni Chuilleanain is a Renaissance scholar at Trinity, and many of her poems deal with evidence of an imperfectly rediscovered past. I find her work a bit more satisfying than McGuckian's simply because her premises are clearer; her ambiguities seem related more to life than to the self-conscious evasions of the poet.

Finally, Seamus Heaney's first collection since winning the Nobel Prize has hardly wanted for comentary, so I will treat it briefly. Opinions about *The Spirit Level* seem evenly divided. Some see in it symptoms of Heaney's decline into slackness and self-parody, while others find him at the top of his game. I'm inclined to the latter view, though I also think Heaney has beeen laureled too soon. He has had to develop too much in the public eye, without the luxury of obscurity, yet he holds still my interest like few other contemporary poets, and I've shrugged off his weaker poems in order to cherish his best. The Heaney I love is not the self-conscious academic, but the poet whose almost Frostian images of work and play go beyond pastoralism, surprising me with sensations of being in the world as it matters most.

Heaney's opening poem, "The Rain Stick," is a rewarding ruse, full of the sounds of water made by "the fall of grit or dry seeds through a cactus." In other words, it's a poem about poetry, the artificial thing that lets us apprehend the real, or so we hope. "You are like a rich man entering heaven/Through the ear of a raindrop," he concludes. "Listen now again." It's a playful, somewhat rueful beginning to a book that contains some rather dark poems, especially the sequence called "Mycenae Lookout":

> ...my whole being rained
>
> Down on myself. I saw cities of grass,
> Valleys of longing, tombs, a wind-swept brightness,
> And far-off, in a hilly, ominous place,
>
> Small crowds of people watching as a man
> Jumped a fresh earth-wall and another ran
> Amorously, it seemed, to strike him down.

When at the end of "Weighing In" Heaney writes, "At this stage only foul play cleans the slate," his usual equanimity vanishes, but he is not a poet who can stay angry for long. "Keeping Going," one of the best poems in the new book, contains yet another grisly killing, the dead man "Feeding the gutter with his copious blood," but it ends by honoring Heaney's brother, who has stayed on in the North after Heaney left, and by recalling their childhood play in which a chair served as a rack of bagpipes:

> My dear brother, you have good stamina.
> You stay on where it happens. Your big tractor
> Pulls up at the Diamond, you wave at people,
> You shout and laugh about the revs, you keep
> Old roads open by driving on the new ones.

You called the piper's sporrans whitewash brushes
And then dressed up and marched us through the kitchen,
But you cannot make the dead walk or right wrong.
I see you at the end of your tether sometimes,
In the milking parlour, holding yourself up
Between two cows until your turn goes past,
Then coming to in the smell of dung again
And wondering, is this all? As it was
In the beginning, is now and shall be?
Then rubbing your eyes and seeing our old brush
Up on the byre door, and keeping going.

This poem is followed by a charming sestina, "Two Lorries," and other poems that make much of his past. I like Heaney's speech-driven meters, at least in the poems where he's in command of them. His success will be held against him, as it always has been, but when I think of my proud Dublin friend saying, "That's the fucker who's going to win the Nobel Prize," I am sure the Swedish Academy could have done worse.

The choices Irish poets now face are the choices faced by poets everywhere: losing themselves in self-referential games and negligent language or trying to engage the public, once again, in the heightened clarities of memorable speech. The fear of seeming merely traditional has to be cast aside in the making of durable poems. The best poets eventually come to believe in an audience of intelligent listeners, not just in decoding critics. Recently, Irish poets have been lucky in their audiences; one hopes they will continue to honor us with poems worth hearing.

---

[1] This essay-review was first published in the spring of 1997.

WEST INDIAN DISCOVERIES

J. Edward Chamberlin's rich introduction to Caribbean poetry in English begins with an appropriate bluntness: "Slavery shaped the West Indies."[1] Immediately we know that this literary historian will not separate aesthetic values from political problems, but will attempt to illuminate them simultaneously. The very first poem he quotes, "Epitaph," by the Jamaican poet Dennis Scott, makes the relationship between history and language harrowingly clear:

> They hanged him on a clement morning, swung
> between the falling sunlight and the women's
> breathing, like a black apostrophe to pain.
> All morning while the children hushed
> their hopscotch joy and the cane kept growing
> he hung there sweet and low.
>   At least that's how
> they tell it. It was long ago
> and what can we recall of a dead slave or two
> except that when we punctuate our island tale
> they swing like sighs across the brutal
> sentences, and anger pauses
> till they pass away.

Professor Chamberlin's eloquent commentary finds in this poem the substance and direction of his entire book. In his view, memory and historical suffering are inseparable from the aesthetic choices poets make. He brings his very substantial knowledge to the case, arguing "that West Indian poets are, willy nilly, at the center of a fundamental poetic issue. The tensions between naturalness and artifice, speech and writing, familiarity and strangeness are in theory sources of strength. In practice, however, they can also be sources of stress." By discussing the poetry of a region that is so clearly post-colonial, in which language and power are so frequently part of the same debate, he raises questions of much wider relevance than the scope of his book would at first suggest.

Lately, the distinction between social understanding and aesthetic value has become quite blurry. The fact that Chamberlin has previously written on Oscar Wilde and on the attitudes of whites toward Native Americans suggests that he has frequently revisited questions of politics and poetics. Though his discussion of matters like slavery and black power movements is deeply sympathetic, it is never simplistic. Chamberlin's open, generous survey seems close to the spirit of the leftist critic, C.L.R. James, who once wrote,

> The West Indian writers have discovered the West Indies and West Indians, a people of the middle of our disturbed century, concerned with the discovery of themselves, determined to discover themselves, but without hatred or malice against the foreigner, even the bitter imperialist past.

That may sound too cosy to be true, but the work of Earl Lovelace, Derek Walcott, Edward Kamau Brathwaite, Lorna Goodison and others seems to bear it out. The Whitmanesque spirit of inclusiveness underlies most of what Chamberlin has to say, while that great misanthrope, V.S. Naipaul, is the bugaboo of nothingness against whom these writers oppose themselves. Theirs is the story of an evolving post-colonial consciousness. Many of us who are not descendants of slaves can understand the problem of growing up far from cultural centers, feeling displaced and rootless. Chamberlin, a Canadian, also seems to feel that this is a global experience. We're all post-colonial. We're all regional. And we're all trying to discover what that means.

But there are limits to this sociological approach toward literature; Chamberlin seems well aware of them when he writes, "Every poet has two allegiances: one to the facts of local experience, and the other to the formalities of literary expression. To life; and to art." In discussing this divided loyalty, Chamberlin reveals that he is skeptical about any theory of universal forms. When he writes of Bartoleme de las Casas, who so famously opposed slavery in the sixteenth century, he concludes, "Las Casas would probably be accused of 'political correctness' these days, for he argued that we must recognize relativities of meaning and value." There is no denying that what anthropologists call "contact" always displays these relativities in sharp relief. In post-colonial narratives, the heroes of the colonizers become the villains of the colonized (just try extolling Churchill to the Irish). Even thoughtful English men of letters like Carlyle and Trollope left a saddening record of racist remarks. Luckily, Chamberlin's point is not that we should stop reading Carlyle and Trollope because of these serious lapses, but that we should face up to the facts of xenophobia and racism that underlie most intercultural contact from Herodotus on down. His history might have been deepened if he had quoted from slave narratives, such as Olaudah Equiano's 1789 autobiography, but Chamberlin wants us to understand the role of European racism in West Indian conceptions of audience and language, how rebellion against the powers of Babylon (to use the Rastafarian term for the white world) lies at the heart of so much Caribbean poetry.

Perhaps his strongest example of the European inability to see any culture but its own derives from the nineteenth-century historian James Anthony Froude, who wrote, "There has been no saint in the West Indies since Las Casas, no hero unless philonegro enthusiasm can make one out of Toussaint. There are no people there in the true sense of the word, with a character and purpose of their own." We are properly shocked by such statements, but we should not forget that modernists like Eliot and Beckett made similar statements about the "hollowness" of modern Europeans. Naipaul has frequently adopted a similar despair, portraying West Indian politicians as "mimic men." One of the many fascinating facts Chamberlin offers is that the emblem of St. Lucia is a parrot—simultaneously local and suggestive of universal anxieties about identity, a voice that mimics the voices of its owners, worse than a slave because a slave can at least rebel in his or her language. West Indian populism is born of such rebellions—calypso, reggae, ska, dub poetry—rejecting modernist despair for the theatre of a new identity.

Language as identity and rebellion. Chamberlin rightly points out that we have seen this before in Scotland and Ireland. In Nigeria, writers like Chinua Achebe are sometimes criticized for mastering a foreign form, the English novel, and not writing enough in Ibo or other local tongues. The triumph of English in so much of the world has created identity crises. Olaudah Equiano, the West African ex-slave, wrote a supple English prose designed to please an eighteenth-century London audience, while many of the modern dialect poems quoted by Chamberlin are as difficult for me to understand as the early Scots of Gawin Douglas. Phonetic spelling in dialect can be tough on a reader, whether Shaw's cockney in *Major Barbara,* or the lyrics of Louise Bennett:

> Me glad fi see yuh come back, bwoy,
> But lawd, yuh let me dung;
> Me shame a yuh so till all a
> Me proudness drop a gung.

Europeans colonized through language as much as by the gun. (In fact, some languages have been preserved by these colonizing efforts, partly in translations of the Bible.) Chamberlin's examples of linguistic colonization are numerous, the following perhaps his most obvious:

> In 1492, when Queen Isabella was proudly presented with the first grammar of Spanish ever written, she asked impatiently, "What is it for?" The answer she got from the Bishop of Seville must have appealed to the woman who sponsored Columbus. "Language is the perfect instrument of empire."

In a modern movie that scene would be played as the epitome of evil. More examples of linguistic coercion range from the Welsh Stone and the Irish hedgerow to the Indian boarding schools of North America—all of which represent attempts to eradicate a local language and replace it with an imperial one. At this point Chamberlin's survey shifts, inevitably, to the language theories of twentieth century Europeans: Saussure, Jakobson, Bakhtin *et al.* His brief discussion of their work is clearly justified and mercifully jargon-free. In order to disarm critics of West Indian populism and dialect poetry, he argues that "The idea of a standard form of the language is a powerful fiction, which among other things represents a hierarchy of prestige and power." In another chapter he quotes Joyce's Stephen Dedalus on the subject:

> The language in which we are speaking is his before it is mine. How different are the words *home, Christ, ale, master,* on his lips and on mine! I cannot speak or write these words without unrest of spirit. His language, so familiar and so foreign, will always be for me an acquired speech. I have not made or accepted its words. My voice holds them at bay. My soul frets in the shadow of his language.

We have reached that point in history when a great many speakers of English in India, Malawi, Nigeria, Kenya, Australia, North America—make your own list—would agree with Stephen Dedalus.

But the loyalties of an artist like Joyce are hard to pin down; he could be as scathing about the Irish as Naipaul is about the Trinidadians. His Gabriel Conroy, taunted as a "West Briton," speaks some of the loveliest English "poetry" around. In short, English is not the property of England, and this has been true for a very long time. Merely to dismiss what Adrienne Rich once called "the oppressor's language" is no solution—languages are not used only to subdue people—and Chamberlin's shrewdest point comes late in the book when he suggests that the language of "the people" is also a fiction, a sophisticated stylization, like all poetry a negotiation between form and speech. If English has been used as a tool of oppression—and I cannot think of any language on earth that has not—it has also been enriched by the creative energies of those who have been oppressed. Throughout its history, English has proved fabulously absorbent and flexible—a great sponge of a language best represented by the swelling imperial edifice of the O.E.D. The instrument of empire is also the vehicle of poetry.

Despite the mongrel nature of the language, one must still argue that some uses of it are better than others. Chamberlin's ambivalence about linguistic hierarchies leaves him little room for aesthetic judgment. In the fifth of his six lengthy chapters, he describes the careers of three poets who, he feels, represent the major accomplishments of the region: Derek Walcott, Edward Kamau Brathwaite and Lorna Goodison. All three poets offer robust versions of poetry's eternal dialogue between life and art, history and forms of expression. Walcott is the most prodigiously talented of the three; Chamberlin frequently refers to the epic poem, *Omeros*, for its post-colonial vision as much as its poetry. Here the weakness of sociological criticism shows. Reviewing *Omeros* a few years back, I criticized Walcott's conflation of several colonial experiences—West African, Irish and Native American—not because it was intellectually false, but because it distracted from his story. At times he appeared to be writing for an audience of professors in some vast department of multicultural studies. I think Walcott writes better when he limits himself to the local (admittedly, given his annual peregrinations, this is hard to define). Nearly all of his attempts to adopt an international pose ring hollow to me, while his poems of St. Lucian or Trinidadian experience, especially those in dialect, are frequently wonderful.

Brathwaite, on the other hand, has largely been a poet of Negritude, translating his African experience (seven years in Ghana) into poems about West Indian identity. While there are powerful passages in his trilogy, *The Arrivants*, I have found few Brathwaite poems that seem to me truly memorable. When he writes that "the hurricane does not howl in pentameters," I can't see that he has made any sort of argument at all. It confuses or ignores the fact of the poet's divided loyalties to art and to life. My reservations about Brathwaite lead me to difficult questions: What is good poetry? What is it for? How do we know it when we see or hear it? Many critics now believe that all aesthetic values are relative. I simply cannot agree, though I recognize that if we are honest our debate will leave plenty of uncertainty. Chamberlin says that poetry ought to help people live their lives, but he forgets to press for the best poems that give the best help through language that is vivid and precise and memorable.

The third of Chamberlin's triad of major poets is Lorna Goodison, whose work was a revelation to me, much of it beautiful for its simple negotiation of the line between life and art. Here is a poem of hers called "The Mulatta as Penelope":

> Tonight, I'll pull your limbs through
> small soft garments
> your head will part my breasts
> and you will hear a different heartbeat.
> Tonight, we said the real goodbye, he and I
> but this time I will not sit and spin and spin
> the door open to let the madness in.
> Till the sailor finally weary of the sea
> returns with tin souvenirs and a claim to me.
> True I returned from the quayside
> my eyes full of sand
> and his salt-leaving smell
> fresh on my hands
> but you're my anchor awhile now
> and that holds deep.
> I'll sit in the sun
> and dry my hair
> while you sleep.

Poems like this one (I'm quoting from the anthology mentioned below rather than the slightly different version in Chamberlin) make a good case for standard English, or at least for its availability, so we can also step outside local experience and speak to many people about the human heart.

I have a few more quibbles with Chamberlin's good book. On page 114 he wrongly suggests that Eliot's ideas about impersonality in poetry came after *The Waste Land* rather than before; on page 244 he quotes Yeats's "Adam's Curse" as though it were prose; and in his thorough bibliography he credits *The Penguin Book of Caribbean Verse in English* to Paul (rather than Paula) Burnett. If I also feel dissatisfied with his account of aesthetic values, perhaps I reveal my own frustration that so many of the poems in this book are quoted for social understanding, so few for breathtaking lines. I liked what I saw of Lorna Goodison, Dennis Scott, Ian McDonald, David Dabydeen and others, but I wonder why the Jamaican-born Edward Lucie-Smith is not found here. Is he considered a British poet now? His poems "Your Own Place" and "Imperialists in Retirement" would have been fine additions to Chamberlin's discussion, and in "The Wise Child" I find an apt conclusion for my review:

> I couldn't wait. My childhood angered me.
> It was a sickness time would cure in time,
> But clocks were doctors slow to make me well.
> I sulked and raged. My parents told me 'play'—
> I stood in the garden shouting my own name.
> The noise enlarged me. I can hear it still.
>
> At last I've come where then I longed to go.
> And what's the change?—I find that I can choose
> To wish for where I started. Childhood puts
> Its prettiest manners on. I see the dew
> Filming the lawn I stamped.
>
> The wise child knows
> Not here, not there, the perfect somewhere waits.

---

[1] A review of *Come Back to Me, My Language: Poetry and the West Indies*, by J. Edward Chamberlin.

LOUIS SIMPSON'S SINGULAR CHARM

They will send me off to Heaven
when all I want is to live in the world.
— "Searching for the Ox"

Louis Simpson was born in Jamaica in 1923, the son of a prominent lawyer and an aspiring opera singer whose family were Russian émigrés. Their marriage ended while Simpson was still in school. The boy who would become a Pulitzer Prize-winning American poet discovered only when he joined his mother in New York that her family were assimilated Jews. This is the rich and confusing identity Simpson has explored throughout his career. His childhood was that of a British colonial and public school boy, but he has adapted in adult life to cosmopolitan New York. His mobility and mixed heritage seem especially New World phenomena. At least one anthology of Caribbean poetry claims him for Jamaica, yet he is well known in the United States as the author of "American Poetry":

> Whatever it is, it must have
> A stomach that can digest
> Rubber, coal, uranium, moons, poems.
>
> Like the shark, it contains a shoe.
> It must swim for miles through the desert
> Uttering cries that are almost human.

Perhaps this little poem is as Pan-American as its author. In his long and productive career, Simpson has touched a main current of contemporary life, and just as often he has spoken of our evolving poetry.

Indeed, the outline of Simpson's life has something both archetypal and singular about it. His was the generation of poets tempered by World War II — an experience that may have helped them see through the cant of much contemporary criticism. They came of age as writers when postwar trauma had given way to — or had simply been overwhelmed by — suburban boom. They expressed poetry's alienation from that environment even as they moved into the university, creating a new kind of social assimilation for poets that was profound in its benefits and drawbacks. Many of these poets experienced the further alienation of divorce, the angry disruptions of the sixties, etc., and many of them abandoned meter and rhyme as they endured these social changes. Among poets, the deep effects of such developments are still debated.

But these facts cannot fully explain the peculiar charm of Simpson's best work. He continually frustrates literary categorization, standing with clear-eyed bemusement at the fringes of contradictory movements. A brief comparison of Simpson to his contemporaries reveals that he has marked out his own literary territory. Richard Wilbur and Anthony Hecht, poets close to Simpson's age who share his war experience, never abandoned traditional verse, and have made some of the finest postwar poems in English. They are now American poetry's elder statesmen, whereas two younger poets, John Ashbery and the late Allen Ginsberg, seem by contrast never to have grown up. Their prolific self-indulgence has resulted in poems that are alike mainly in their dullness. Listening to a recording of Ginsberg reading "Howl," I suddenly realized that he sounded as monotonous as a Conehead from the old "Saturday Night Live." Ashbery is capable of charm, but so often displays his indifference to the audience that any sensible reader would respond with a like indifference. The one time I heard Ashbery read (to a weirdly adoring hometown crowd in Rochester, New York), I wondered whether the poet would nod off before I did. The grossly inflated reputations of Ashbery and Ginsberg loom over contemporary American poetry; one can only hope that withering time will reduce their trunkloads of published work to chapbooks worthy of the art.

Simpson is unlike any of these poets because he writes coherent narratives in free verse. Neither a seer nor, finally, a traditional maker, Simpson writes out of a prose sensibility much like Chekhov's, noting the comic absurdity and pathos of ordinary lives. Comparing him to still more poets born in the 1920s—Donald Justice, Donald Hall, Adrienne Rich, James Wright, Galway Kinnell, Robert Bly, etc.—only illustrates again how Simpson, while very much of his time, remains apart. To write about his life, one must also address his work, and the most significant aspect of that has been the development of his own contradictory attitudes toward forms of expression.

Simpson's rejection of meter must be placed in this historical context. While Wilbur, Hecht and others continued to make durable poems, a whole range of writers found meter incompatible with their vision of modern life. Meter is measure, a kind of compression that, in the right hands, lends language a supercharged memorability. In the wrong hands it sounds as mechanical as a player piano. Poets like Bly and Kinnell rejected meter before they had demonstrated any ability to make genuine use of it. No doubt their goals were in some way laudable, but legions of their followers have narrowed their poetics even further. I remember editors telling me in the 1980s that alliteration was "too rich" for contemporary poetry, as if we were all henceforth sentenced to a diet of bread and water. Of course generalizations are always unjust, but I can't help agreeing with Donald Hall when he finds much contemporary poetry lacking in ambition. In too many cases, the abandonment of a full range of auditory possibilities represents an abandonment of real standards.

I don't think this is true of Louis Simpson, however. Like Hall, he has consistently been an engaging and candid critic, keeping the idea of ambition alive while others fed slops to the bairns. Reading through Simpson's *Collected Poems* (1988), one finds a poet who has never written merely for critics or in self-congratulation, a poet who cares enough about readers to give them memorable moments. Among his early metrical poems, I like "Carentan O Carentan," "The Battle," "The Man Who Married Magdalene" and especially "To the Western World":

> A siren sang, and Europe turned away
> From the high castle and the shepherd's crook.
> Three caravels went sailing to Cathay
> On the strange ocean, and the captains shook
> Their banners out across the Mexique Bay.
>
> And in our early days we did the same.
> Remembering our fathers in their wreck
> We crossed the sea from Palos where they came
> And saw, enormous to the little deck,
> A shore in silence waiting for a name.

The treasures of Cathay were never found.
In this America, this wilderness
Where the axe echoes with a lonely sound,
The generations labor to possess
And grave by grave we civilize the ground.

Simpson quotes that memorable final stanza in his memoir, *The King My Father's Wreck,* a book that movingly revisits his life and art. The poet of "To the Western World" and the blank verse narrative "The Runner" (so influential to younger narrative poets working now) has undergone a metamorphosis. One might say the butterfly has chosen to become a caterpillar:

> There was no precedent for the kind of poetry I wanted to write. Some years ago I had broken with rhyme and meter and learned to write in free form. Now I discarded the traditional ornaments of language, especially metaphors. I wanted to render the thing itself exactly as it happened.

Simpson received the Pulitzer precisely at that moment when the transformation of his verse had begun, with his ironic take on Walt Whitman: "The Open Road goes to the used car lot." Though he has produced intriguing poetry in the years since, he has also courted danger, choosing a slighter technical range that often highlights his lackadaisical diction.

The pursuit of directness in poetry is not new, of course. Wordsworth famously announced that "Poets do not write for Poets alone, but for men." Simpson describes the audience he sought as follows:

> They married and lived in houses; they had children, drove cars, went to work, shopped in supermarkets, and watched TV. Poetry hardly ever spoke of this. .. it did not speak of such lives except with irony and contempt. But I was one of those people... the only thing that made me different was being a writer. I wanted to speak of the life I had and tell stories about the men and women I knew. The stories would be in verse, for this was what I enjoyed . . . the rhythm of the line.

Here is Wordsworth again:

> If it be affirmed that rhyme and metrical arrangement of themselves
> constitute a distinction which overturns what has just been said on
> the strict affinity of metrical language with that of prose, and paves
> the way for other artificial distinctions which the mind voluntarily
> admits, I answer that the language of such Poetry as is here recom-
> mended is, as far as possible, a selection of the language really spo-
> ken by men; that this selection, wherever it is made with true taste
> and feeling, will of itself form a distinction far greater than would at
> first be imagined, and will entirely separate the composition from
> the vulgarity and meanness of ordinary life; and, if metre be
> superadded thereto, I believe that a dissimilitude will be produced
> altogether sufficient for the gratification of a rational mind.

Both Wordsworth and Simpson know that real poets give pleasure. Both believe in using a "selection" of the language of men,
and both know the importance of taste and feeling, though they
would differ where vulgarity is concerned. Simpson often avoids
meter, and he approaches realms of experience Wordsworth never
dreamed could be suitable for a poem. Witness the opening two
stanzas of "How to Live on Long Island":

> Lilco, $75.17;
> Mastercard, $157.89;
> Sunmark Industries, $94.03...
>
> Jim is paying his bills.
> He writes out a check
> and edges it into the envelope
> provided by the company.
> They always make them too small.

This deliberate banality signals, as Simpson has said of other
poets, a revolution in taste. My question remains a simple one: Has
this revolution been good for poetry? Despite my affection for poems like "Physical Universe," a brilliant suburban collage, I have
to say that Simpson's technique leaves disturbing implications for
the art.

In fact, though Simpson wrote some fine poems in meter, he now seems almost willfully to misunderstand it. He loves Chaucer and many other English, Irish, Scots and American poets who have worked in fixed forms, but he comes close to that tired solecism that meter is un-American. His new book of essays, *Ships Going into the Blue*, contains an example of this. "An American View of Pasternak" offers the following averment from the Russian poet:

> "I have never understood those dreams of a new language, of a completely original form of expression. Because of this dream, much of the work of the twenties was merely stylistic experimentalism and has ceased to exist. The most extraordinary discoveries are made when the artist is overwhelmed by what he has to say. In his urgency he uses the old language, and the old language is transformed from within."

Pasternak's statement seems to me the soul of wisdom, but Simpson responds that "The mainstream of American writing, as of American life, is 'formal experiment.'" Well, others before me have pointed out that mainstream American poetry is hardly experimental in its domestication of free verse. A few sentences later, Simpson makes the all-too-common mistake of assuming that Emerson's famous call for a "metre-making argument" connotes approval of free verse. In fact, Emerson's meaning is much closer to Pasternak's; good work in meter is driven by the urgency of argument and emotion.

Moments like this recur in Simpson's prose, and I find irritating passages in the verse as well. Because of his stance toward poetry, he can fall into facile phrasings that spoil whole poems. One needn't be banal in expressing banality. A poem like "The Pawnshop" is true in its way, but its conclusion is no more memorable than the average New Age handbook: "Each has its place in the universe." Simpson has worked terribly hard, it would seem, to create an aurally impoverished poetry.

These criticisms are important if we want to understand how and when Simpson's poems succeed. In his best free verse, one has the feeling of deliberately chosen language, a trained ear measuring lines by intuition and long practice:

> There is something in disorder that calls to me.
> Out there beyond the harbor
> where, every night, the lighthouse
> probes the sea with its feathery beam,
> something is rising to the surface.

Still, his delight in disorder lacks the precision of Robert Herrick—note how he repeats the filler word "something" in the above passage from the sequence called "Searching for the Ox." Both grammar and attitude become passive; the reporter nearly subdues the poet.

As I said at the beginning of this essay, Simpson's successes and failures are particularly his, yet also unthinkable at any other point in literary history. Both public trends and private life have driven this restless search for a new form. In "Working Late," one of his best poems, I sense the shaping hand of an artist closing in on his true subjects:

> A light is on in my father's study.
> "Still up?" he says, and we are silent,
> looking at the harbor lights,
> listening to the surf
> and the creak of coconut boughs.
>
> He is working late on cases.
> No impassioned speech! He argues from evidence,
> actually pacing out and measuring,
> while the fans revolving on the ceiling
> winnow the true from the false.
>
> Once he passed a brass curtain rod
> through a head made out of plaster
> and showed the jury the angle of fire—
> where the murderer must have stood.
>
> For years, all through my childhood,
> if I opened a closet. . . bang!
> There would be the dead man's head
> with a black hole in the forehead.

All the arguing in the world
will not stay the moon.
She has come all the way from Russia
to gaze for a while in a mango tree
and light the wall of a veranda,
before resuming her interrupted journey
beyond the harbor and the lighthouse
at Port Royal, turning away
from land to the open sea.

Yet, nothing in nature changes, from that day to this,
she is still the mother of us all.
I can see the drifting offshore lights,
black posts where the pelicans brood.

And the light that used to shine
at night in my father's study
now shines as late in mine.

Though he finds universal feeling in this personal experience —
and in a language of beautiful simplicity — I can't help noticing how
good free verse often settles into metered lines at key points, as in
the concluding trimeters of the poem.

Simpson quotes "Working Late" to conclude an especially sad
chapter in *The King My Father's Wreck*. Just as the poem shifts subtly in time and space, associating the father's measured work and
the mother's mystery with the speaker's own labors, the new memoir feels out a direction, its time scheme intuitive and nonlinear.
The charm of both works derives from the confidence of the writer,
the shaping sensibility almost invisible in the text. This excellent
book circles its subjects — parents, past events, lost friends, a new
marriage — suddenly revealing key pieces of information that illuminate everything that has come before them.

The chapter in which Simpson quotes "Working Late" begins
with a startling revelation: "When our father died and the will was
read my brother and I had been disinherited. He had left us a few
hundred pounds — the rest of his large estate went to our stepmother.
She had arranged matters so, and the day after the funeral she sent

us packing." The pain of disinheritance haunts Simpson's work, and in the memoir his technique is particularly effective. Describing his parents' separation and his mother's departure for New York, he adds, "This was the great blow of my life, and it occurred in silence." He sees clearly how this trauma contributed to the kind of artist he became:

> I buried my anguish deep, and there it would remain, "A grief without a pang, vast, void, and drear." It would affect my life, especially my relations with women, but it harmed my imagination too, for you cannot suppress one part of feeling without suppressing others.

The flat, declarative nature of much of his writing may have originated in a kind of shell shock that predates the war:

> I would see my mother again. One afternoon I went with my father to a house near the sea, at Bournemouth, that he was thinking of buying. It wasn't finished, it was littered with sawdust and wood. We were standing in the middle of an empty room when my mother appeared in the doorway. She was holding a pistol and pointing it at him. "Rosalind," he said, and walked across the room and took it from her hand. She fell to the floor and shrieked, frothing at the mouth.

Memory of family life often resembles memory of war, and *The King My Father's Wreck* contains many losing battles; its opening anecdote locates the ironic place of Waterloo in his boyhood imagination: "Like Thackeray I'm at a bit of a loss to know what it adds up to, fact and fiction, things that have happened and things I've read about or seen in movies." A lifelong stand-off with his father's imposing ghost underlies everything else he tells us about his Jamaican youth, the war, struggles to establish a career and recent travels. In his longest chapter, "The Vigil," Simpson visits his dying mother in Italy; he obsessively catalogues daily activities like sports and sightseeing, and we soon realize that they are diversions to keep him from focusing on the impending death. He struggles to live in the world, to enjoy himself, and sometimes he seems actually to succeed, but this avoidance of emotion surely suggests the old childhood wounds — exacerbated, perhaps, by the psychological toll of later combat. He allows his readers to discover for themselves what he is up to; the book's understatement lets us feel time's passage and the shape-changing presences that dominate memory. *The King My Father's Wreck* is, ultimately, a profound record of tenacity and love.

His new book of essays, *Ships Going into the Blue,* seems more haphazard, with the catchall quality most essay collections have, but it still makes absorbing reading. Simpson has published two earlier collections in the University of Michigan's "Poets on Poetry" series: *A Company of Poets* (1981) and *The Character of the Poet* (1986). In all three collections (unlike earlier prose books, *Three* on *the Tower* and *A Revolution in Taste*), occasional pieces rub shoulders with a few more substantial essays. Simpson's criticism is often refreshingly personal, as if we were overhearing after-dinner opinions on a variety of subjects. I've already said that I disagree with some of his ideas, and *Ships Going into the Blue* offers still more occasions for such disagreement, usually over trivial matters like the effect of word processing on literary composition (Simpson fails to see that the word processor has not made writing any easier at all — only typing), but the book also contains many fine and readable pieces I expect I will return to.

Even in brief reviews one finds good insights, like this one about Robinson Jeffers:

> Grandeur has gone out of our view of things. Other qualities have taken their place—humor for one. But the note we heard in the *Old Testament?* In Milton and *Lear?* Jeffers had it in him, and when he was touched, and wasn't pontificating, he could write poetry of a kind, towering—the word suggests itself—that we have not had in America since.

This passage describes elements lacking in Simpson's own verse. Such catholicity of taste, the ability to appreciate writers unlike oneself, is the mark of a truly humane reader. Brief memoirs published here, "Humane Letters" and "Theatre Business," illuminate Simpson's times, and essays like "'The Precinct Station'—Structure and Idea" have sensible things to say about revision. His note-book entry on Postmodernism is one of the best short discussions of that baffling phenomenon I know, and his concluding lecture, "Thoughts about a Doubtful Enterprise," proves an important document concerning poetry's relation to a civil culture. Here Simpson demonstrates that he does not believe merely in recording the world as it is, but also in the transformative power of the imagination. He would probably make no apologies for the contradictions of his career, however, and future anthologists will have to determine the effect of such contradictions on the poems he leaves behind.

These books have one chapter in common, the tiny piece called "A Window," apparently set in the poet's study on Long Island. It is so brief that I may as well quote it whole:

> Breezy and cold, a sun like a diamond blazing so that you can't look at it... the trees and hedge in front of my window are dark shapes. When I think that every day of my life I look at the sky and earth directly, it's a blessing.
>
> It says to me, Write! But it doesn't say what about. That is where nature leaves off, cuts the towline . . . where work starts and those who can't do it fall astern. Up ahead are great ships going into the blue.
>
> Miriam comes back from the walk she takes every afternoon and stops by my study to press her face to the glass and make a mouth like a goldfish. These are the whims that make life worth living. There are people who know this, and then there are the others who provide us with our daily quota of bad news.
>
> Aristotle said that humanity is the animal that lives in a *polis*. How about, the animal that makes faces?

That deflating humor, that earthbound understatement with its paradoxical belief in directness and imagination, seems to me the essence of Louis Simpson's singular charm.

ANNE SEXTON AND HER TIMES

The most rewarding literary biographies rise above the documentary nature of the genre to become works of literature themselves. One need not look all the way back to Boswell for an example. I think of Troyat on Tolstoy, Ellmann on Joyce, and to a lesser degree Carpenter on Auden or Judd on Ford Madox Ford. These books succeed partly by their prose styles and an almost novelistic empathy with their subjects. Diane Wood Middlebrook's biography of Anne Sexton is honest, workmanlike and frequently judicious. There are eloquent passages in this book, but you would never guess that its author is herself a poet. Though Ms. Middlebrook has been professional in every way, she has produced a biography that only sketchily explains the phenomena of Anne Sexton and her times.

For surely Anne Sexton was and is a phenomenon. Her rapid rise and fall, the broad appeal (and sales) of her books nearly twenty years after her suicide, and the notoriety and bestsellerdom of this biography seem peculiarly American. In no other country and at no other time than ours would the psychological—some would say therapeutic—poems of Anne Sexton have taken on such cultural force. Middlebrook is well aware of this when she writes,

> It was the accepted notion of the "abnormality" or "social insignificance" of women's experience as a subject for art that made Plath's themes of rage and vengeance so heady a model for young writers, especially women, and in America, at least, this insight fueled a social movement in which grassroots feminism was the theory, grassroots poetry the practice. Among students and among women readers, Plath and Sexton were necessary aids to understanding hysteria as resistance to social programming. Consequently, writing poetry in the manner of Plath and Sexton became a mode of consciousness-raising. Thus what a poetry reviewer might dismiss as morbid self-preoccupation, another interested reader might welcome as liberating candor. Women poets and critics, of course, had the most at stake in deciding which kind of reader to be, for gender would always be perceived as salient in their case.

This is one of several passages where Middlebrook demonstrates a firm command of the contexts in which Sexton's poems are read, but I wish she had gone further, fully exploring the implications of Sexton's career. For example, she might have asked whether "hysteria" really is resistance to social programming, or whether "candor" really has much to do with what Sexton actually wrote.

Middlebrook is very good at describing the various groups of "confessional" poets who rose to prominence in the early 1960s. Sexton met Sylvia Plath in Robert Lowell's workshop at Harvard in 1959, and both women found acceptance (Sexton more than Plath) at a time when the poet's personal anguish was expected to be a frequent subject of poetry. We now know a great deal about the private lives and sufferings of these people, but Middlebrook also understands the peculiar romanticism with which poets like Plath, Berryman and Sexton dramatized their troubles. I know of no compelling evidence that poets are more susceptible to mental illness or addiction than doctors or lawyers or street sweepers or accountants, yet writers like Sexton perpetuated the myth of the mad, alienated poet. In his 1964 book, *The Far Field*, Theodore Roethke wrote. "What's madness but nobility of soul/At odds with circumstance?" But madness is madness, every bit as specific as a broken femur; there is nothing noble about it. Anne Sexton was not sick in precisely the same way that Plath or Lowell or Roethke or Berryman were sick, yet all of them lived in a time that made it possible to lump these illnesses together under the rubric of poetry.

If there are people who have borne physical and mental illness with heroism, Anne Sexton does not seem to have been one of them. She used people relentlessly, abused her children terribly. Indeed, Middlebrook's biography leaves me feeling much more sympathy for Sexton's family than for Sexton herself. Kayo, her "husband straight as a redwood," put up with more appalling behavior than Sexton had any right to expect, and his frustrated violence, usually under the influence of alcohol, is sad. Because of this biography, the world now knows that Sexton sexually abused her daughter, Linda. For the first years of her two daughters' lives, Sexton hardly lived under the same roof with them, either because she couldn't bear to look at them or she had been shuffled off for treatment somewhere. One quickly loses count of Sexton's suicide attempts and infidelities. To be fair, she seems to have understood her own problems rather well, but ultimately they defeated her, and I also think they defeated most of her poetry.

She was from an early age more a patient than an agent (which is not to say she was undesigning), born to an upper-middle-class family with what seems to me a fairly typical experience of mental instability and social hypocrisy. One of the major drawbacks of Middlebrook's biography is that she races through the first twenty-seven years of Sexton's life at a rate of about ten pages per decade, so family history and milieu become a confusing jumble of names and places. Sexton comes alive only when she is "reborn" as a poet on page 42.

Part of the problem. I suspect, is that Middlebrook had access to material few biographers ever see, including the controversial tapes provided by Sexton's psychiatrist. Dr. Martin Orne. Paradoxically, the wealth of documentary material at Middlebrook's disposal has resulted in literary impoverishment, preventing her from fully imagining her subject's life or filling in more of its cultural background, and as a result Sexton too often seems distant and unsympathetic. Too many passages in this book read like case history:

> The normal development of Linda and Joy into little beings demanding to be let go and nevertheless to be loved unconditionally may have broken the dam that held such a flood in place. These babies were supposed to provide Sexton's fulfillment as a woman, but instead they made demands on her emotions: rather than feeding her hunger for acceptance, they required her to respond to their separateness. As an adult she was supposed to be able to participate intuitively in this exchange, as intuitively as her children did. But what was involuntarily called into play by their demands was her own neediness. Sexton expressed this conflict at first in bodily suffering, later in plain language to her doctor: "I want to be a child and not a mother, and I feel guilty about this."

It was Dr. Orne who encouraged Sexton to write poetry when she was an ill and discontented housewife. Her early poems were therapeutic exercises that Sexton was shrewd enough not to publish. A televised lecture on sonnets by I. A. Richards awakened her latent talent for verse forms, which was reinforced by years of workshops with John Holmes, Maxine Kumin, George Starbuck, W. D. Snodgrass and Robert Lowell. Despite John Holmes's objections to Sexton's self-dramatizations, these workshops apparently provided her with no alternative to confessionalism. In one of her most famous poems from *All My Pretty Ones* (1962) she wrote, "My friend, my friend, I was born/doing reference work in sin, and born/confessing it." Most art is in some way personal. but Sexton's illness was so given to solipsism, her entire life constructed around her needs before anyone else's, that one would think confessional poetry was precisely the wrong kind of poetry for her to be encouraged to write. In a letter to me which I have his permission to quote, Anthony Hecht relates that he once gave Sexton a copy of Aubrey's *Brief Lives* "in the hope of diverting her from her obsessive narcissism." Hecht was not alone in wishing Sexton would discover the world beyond her own problems, but it was not in the cards. Sexton was an actress, a compulsive self-dramatizer, and even if her art raises our consciousness of important social and psychological issues, it is severely compromised by the limits of her personality.

Her 1965 poem, "Suicide Note," responds to the charge of narcissism by quoting Artaud: "You speak to me of narcissism but I reply that it is a matter of my life." She is right, in a way, just as we would be right to recognize the insufficiency of her answer. Maxine Kumin has argued that the value of Sexton's poetry lies in its apparent openness to subjects previously deemed unsuitable for poetry. But choice of subject matter is by itself a poor criterion for aesthetic judgment. Once the shock value of Sexton's choices has worn away, we still have to determine what sort of writer she was. To attempt this, I set out to read Sexton's *Complete Poems* straight through. but the monotony of poem after poem screaming *"me me me"* in lines that were too often flaccid and cliched defeated my best efforts. Sexton is a poet to be taken in small doses.

There are two primary views of her poetry. The first is that she was a poet whose wild subject matter required the taming discipline of rhyme and meter; therefore, her first two books contain her best work and the others, in which free verse predominates. fall away into self-parody. The second view is that she was so honest in her self-analysis that the relentless truths of her subject matter could not be helped by the sedative of traditional form: therefore it is later books like *The Awful Rowing Toward God*, written in roughly twenty days, that give us the real thing. Both of these readings are inaccurate, though I do think much of her best writing comes in the early books. *To Bedlam and Part Way Back* and *All My Pretty Ones* frequently have the virtues of good literary diaries combined with a genuine delight in language. Here, for example is a stanza from her poem "The Double Image":

> There was a church where I grew up
> with its white cupboards where they locked us up,
> row by row, like puritans or shipmates
> singing together. My father passed the plate.
> Too late to be forgiven now, the witches said.
> I wasn't exactly forgiven. They had my portrait
> done instead.

Her playful derangement of images is at the service of a narrative, the diary of an illness. Because of this, the issue of illness seems more at stake than the ego of the patient.

A few poems, like "The Truth the Dead Know," which opens *All My Pretty Ones*, succeed all the way through. But from the start of her career Sexton's poetry exhibited tendencies that detract even from her best work. She frequently begins with an arresting image or stanza, but fails to work out its implications in the rest of the poem. Particularly in the later books, the poems read like promising rough drafts that were left unfinished. Often her poems feel out a direction in sequences of short lyrics, a formal approach that highlights the arresting image at the expense of ideas or sustained dramas.

Transformations, her 1971 revision of traditional fairy tales, offered a reprieve from self-obsession. As Perrault's fairy tales are thinly disguised satires, Sexton's are playful correlatives of therapy — sexuality games. Middlebrook tells us that Sexton had been reading Vonnegut, and poems like "Snow White and the Seven Dwarfs," "Rapunzel" and "Cinderella" have some of Vonnegut's headlong satirical style, as well as a world-weary, enchantment. The poems fall short when like bad Vonnegut, they become too glib. Nevertheless, *Transformations*, coming relatively late in Sexton's career, suggested a way for her to broaden her range. The book became a libretto for Conrad Susa's successful opera, proving that there were several directions in which a poet with Sexton's talents might have gone. But while the intellectual and technical limitations of confessionalism weakened her art, everything else in her life pointed relentlessly to self-destruction.

In his "Foreword" to this biography, Dr. Orne asserts that he could have saved Anne Sexton. I wonder. Surely her prospects were weakened when, after leaving Orne's care, she began a long affair with another therapist. One friend of hers noted that "She couldn't cross the street without getting advice." She was a very sick person, a manic-depressive with powerful neuroses, living on and off Thorazine for the last eight years of her life, her purse a veritable druggist's armamentarium. She was kept afloat by the good will of others, until that good will was exhausted or overcome by her will to die.

Yet reading Middlebrook's book, one finds on page after page testimony to Sexton's vivaciousness. She attracted so many men and women, and in a few of the photographs here she seems as beautiful as their memories attest. But my prevailing sense on closing the book is of someone desperately clutching and clawing at life, one of those poor people on whom death has staked an early claim, so it's a wonder they live as long as they do. Middlebrook fails to make me understand why so many people were and are attracted to Anne Sexton. In fact, I wonder if Middlebrook wasn't herself a bit worn out by her subject. Of the later poetry she writes that "the poet had been survived by the performer."

There are enough felicitous observations in this biography to make me wish there had been more. Summing up Sexton's early crises in relation to her poetry, Middlebrook writes, "July 1960 marked the fourth anniversary of her first hospitalization—the normal length of a college education." I would have liked more of this, as well as a forceful vision of what Sexton's career means and has meant. Instead we have a cautious exposition of the life and work by someone who understands the issues involved but refuses to commit to them, one way or the other. Finally, Anne Sexton is one of too many American poets remembered less for the beauty or rightness of language than for the audacity of a botched life. She was an enormously talented writer who started late and never really found her way, and I wish Middlebrook's book had been better at showing us why.

Short Subjects

J. V. CUNNINGHAM

Though by no means unrecognized in his lifetime, Cunningham's work is not as widely read as it deserves to be. When he is praised it is usually by calling him "our greatest epigrammatist," as if the epigram could never seriously threaten calcified literary hierarchies. It is remarked that he is abstract, dry, bitter, that his oeuvre is small and, at first glance, insubstantial. What critics too seldom notice is that Cunningham is a poet (he preferred to be called a verse-maker) whose vision is as complex as those of T. S. Eliot and Robert Lowell. Cunningham confronts the modern world—its incongruities, its apparent emptiness, its loss—with directness and a purifying anger. Toward the end of his life he said in an interview, "I have no religious beliefs," yet his vision requires the existence of Catholicism, the logic of its authorities, to be understood. The list of what Cunningham rejected would be longer than what he could hold onto; he had no appetite for cant or the superfluous word, and he ruthlessly edited his work. Because of this, Cunningham can be read as a kind of antidote to the more self-satisfied poets of our age.

He was born on August 23, 1911, in Cumberland, Maryland, and when only a few years old moved with his family to Billings, Montana. Because of this move, he knew little about his mother's Irish Catholic family. His father was a construction worker, also of Irish Catholic descent. In Billings, Cunningham went with his brothers to St. Vincent's Parochial School. He spent summers on a nearby ranch, a period alluded to in his poem, "Montana Fifty Years Ago." When he was twelve his family moved to Denver, where he finished the eighth grade at St. Elizabeth's School on Tennyson Street and the next fall entered a Jesuit high school. Having skipped two grades early on, Cunningham was graduated from high school at the age of sixteen and went to work at various Denver newspapers. His father had died suddenly the year before in an industrial accident. Cunningham referred to the Market Crash of 1929 as "the dominant experience of my life." In an important interview with the poet Timothy Steele, he details the years of hard luck, wandering throughout the southwest looking for work while educating himself in modern poetry. His early education had emphasized the classics, yet by the age of eighteen he had encountered all the major modernists and, at what some would call an opposite literary pole, the poems of Jonathan Swift.

There had been abortive attempts at college, and finally Cunningham, with the help of Yvor Winters, went to Stanford University, taking his A.B. in 1934 and his Ph.D. eleven years later. Cunningham had studied both the classics and mathematics—he taught math at a military base in World War II—but he settled on English as his academic discipline. Though in 1957 Winters dedicated his book, *The Function of Criticism,* to Cunningham, his influence on the younger poet's career may be overstressed. Certainly Cunningham expressed gratitude for Winters' help, and for a while the two even shared the same publisher, Alan Swallow. But Winters rightly pointed out that Cunningham possessed his own mind and might have been led to Renaissance studies by W. D. Briggs and the love of Ben Jonson's verse as much as anything else. In addition, Cunningham showed little appetite for the sort of canon-making criticism in which Winters was engaged; for the most part, he divided his attentions between Renaissance scholarship and the revision of his poems. He taught at a number of universities, including Harvard and the University of Virginia, before settling at Brandeis in 1953. There were awards: two Guggenheim Fellowships and others from the National Institute of Arts and Letters and the Academy of American Poets. Cunningham was married three times; by his first marriage to Barbara Gibbs, he fathered one daughter; his second marriage to Dolora Gallagher was childless; in 1950 he married Jessie MacGregor, with whom he lived until his death on March 28, 1985.

Cunningham's scholarship is characterized by astute textual readings and an interest in literary style balanced by careful historical interpretation. Scholarship offered Cunningham a way out of the self, an outlet for affections that do not often surface in his poetry. In the essay "The Quest of the Opal," he writes about himself in the third person, in what he calls "a chastity of diction and a crispness of technique," as if the self were finally nothing more than one of discourse's "devices."

This is where Cunningham's inability to believe on faith alone is given its most forthright explication. Catholicism suggests less a social identity than a method of argument derived largely from Thomas Aquinas. In Cunningham's work, the relentless logic and consideration of alternative positions create a consciousness of fictions and significations, with a residue of disconnected anger. As he wrote in "The Journal of John Cardan," "a man must live divided against himself: only the selfishly insane can integrate experience to the heart's desire, and only the emotionally sterile would not wish to."

If there is a Cunningham persona, a typical figure who suffers and taunts us in the poems, it would be mistaken to call him emotionally sterile. That he can find "no virtue, except in sinuous exacting speech" by itself suggests that virtue is something he has sought and failed to find in himself and the rest of humanity. In "Timor Dei" he rejects the Catholicism with which he was raised, yet he admits that what he fears most is absolute fear, a God without confidence. Wit, in this context, is a bitter joy, an attempt to compensate for inconsolable loss. Cunningham's reliance upon reason is almost pathological; he mistrusts paradox, yet he seems simultaneously aware that reason's solutions, like the proofs of mathematical theorems, are finally rhetorical. His small poem, "Montana Pastoral," as much as Eliot's *Waste Land*, suggests that the conventions of elegy have failed to demonstrate the actual depletion of meaning from existence.

> I am no shepherd of a child's surmises.
> I have seen fear where the coiled serpent rises.
>
> Thirst where the grasses burn in early May
> And thistle, mustard, and the wild cat stay.
>
> There is dust in this air. I saw in the heat
> Grasshoppers busy in the threshing wheat.
>
> So to this hour. Through the warm dusk I drove
> To blizzards sifting on the hissing stove,
>
> And found no images of pastoral will,
> But fear, thirst, hunger, and this huddled chill.

Finally, in a sequence like *Doctor Drink*, man is reduced to his ugliest state, isolate, a sophist drowning in his own bile.

It is usual at such moments to stress the redemption of art, but, enjoyable as his poems are, Cunningham makes no redemptive claim. Perhaps this is why he is at his best when he criticizes our illusions about love and poetry. With regard to poetic form, for example, he easily dismisses the prevalent notion that metrical regularity is meaningless. While most contemporary poets write as though free verse and a sort of watered-down imagism were law, Cunningham is unafraid of the metered line and the pithy abstraction. Yet it is not true that his verse offers no sensuous images and textures. His beautiful sequence *To What Strangers, What Welcome* is full of them.

Cunningham is, among other things, one of our best poets about the western landscape. He sees it as a pared, difficult place where no mirage can solidify—a landscape, as it were, abstracted, yet real and worn by its being. This is the landscape one imagines behind even his most philosophical poems; it is the bony grimace behind his epigrams about love and sex. Cunningham is the kind of poet who disproves our critical categories; working in the rigorous tradition of Martial and stressing the plain style of Cicero, or that of Ben Jonson, he is among the most "modern" of our poets.

THOMAS MCGRATH

When we speak highly of political poetry we usually mean poetry that opposes someone else's point of view. Political poets are valued for the valor of their pronouncements; if their cause is just, their poems are important. Unfortunately, history has a way of complicating things. As the late Terrence Des Pres put it, "Political events . . . can discredit in a day the hard-held convictions of a lifetime" (he was writing about Brecht). Much political poetry is occasional, and the immediate significance of the occasion is supposed to excuse the poet's lame expressions, vanity, sentimentality, blindness or outright lies. It is too easy for political poets to be bad writers, preening before the self-created image of their own righteousness. Nevertheless, I have sometimes found myself bored by poets for whom little was at stake. When the accuracy, memorability or beauty of language quickened my interest, I frequently discovered that I was also reading poetry of social significance. This poetry suggested that words had meaning in relation to actual events, to a world in which few people vote and fewer read good writing. Good political poetry, I decided, is good poetry that includes politics.

Though Thomas McGrath has often been called a political poet, the appellation is imprecise. Certainly politics delayed his recognition by the literary establishment (McGrath must be the most famous neglected poet of recent decades). When he died in September 1990, his work was receiving greater attention than ever, but I would argue that he deserved more. When I finally read through all of his verse (I haven't read the novels, filmscripts, children's books, etc.), I came away feeling that here was the real thing. He wrote a lot of political poems, some good, some awful, but what survives in the work is more complicated than anyone's party line: a voice that is both extraordinarily beautiful and exasperatingly uneven. McGrath would never win awards for neatness, but he had a formal and intellectual reach that beggars the work of many more famous poets. He was both *engagé* and academic, populist bard and recondite craftsman, even a formalist—which is to say he worked well in a variety of forms. The loose hexameters of *Letter to an Imaginary Friend* might have made a fine translation of Homer. He could write gorgeous lyrics like "The World of the Perfect Tear" or "The Bread of This World," poems suggesting a range of influences far broader than is implied by the usual comparisons to Whitman. His compassionate anger and verbal play are what I remember most; reading his best poems I catch echoes of Dante, Chaucer, Hopkins, Joyce, Crane, MacNeice, Thomas—even the "Eliot Auden" he made fun of in "Ars Poetica."

I could go on. The publication of *Death Song*, McGrath's last collection, is bound to summon up eulogistic praise. Luckily for us, it is a reasonably good book, though it represents his faults along with his strengths. Equally composed of small, epigrammatic poems and longer lyrics, *Death Song* is McGrath's most autumnal work. The invective for which he is justly known has softened in his preparation for death:

And so, in the imperial extension of the dark,
Against which, all my life, I opposed my body,
I long to pass from this anguish of passings
Into the calm of an indifferent joy .

To enter October's frail canoe and drift down
Down with the bright leaves among the raucous wildfowl
On the narrowing autumn river where, in these longer nights,
Secretly, in the shallows or on reedy shorelines,
Ice is already forming.

In this poem, "Longing," he came close to predicting the moment when he would die. But though the book is McGrath's own death song, it takes note of other deaths as well. "Slaughterhouse Music," for example, evokes both the ignominious fate of cattle and the darkest chapters in human history without a single shrill or self-serving moment:

The black gate opens on its shuddering hinge.
Our first contingent is cut out and enters.
The door swings...
But not before we hear a dull thudding
As of mauls
On wood stumps muffled by animal skins ...
And we see the flash of axes, rising and falling,
Like puny lightning in the heavy gloom ...
The door swings shut before we might race in and stop it—
If we could or if we would.
But we still hear and see—as if in dream.
And so we begin to sing.

In other poems, McGrath expresses outrage at what he sees as the grinding banality of American life, but his writing about revolution, as in a little poem called "Than Never," can be utterly foolish: "When you wake anywhere to gunfire and revolution/You'll know you're there./Late!/But not too late." Just what is the poet's attitude here? Are these lines intended to imply that shooting people will solve our many problems? He doesn't say, and his not saying is irresponsible. When he is in full command of his thought, feeling and wit—as in the Audenesque song, "End of a Season," or "The

Crippled Artist" or "Legends, Heroes, Myth Figures and Other American Liars"—a fuller humanity emerges. Here are some good lines, expressive of their author's faith, from "Working in Darkness":

> I think of the ones like the poet John Haines,
> During those long years in Alaska,
> Working alone in a cold place,
> Sitting in the darkness outside the pool of light:
> Ice-Fisherman facing the empty hole of the page,
> Patient, the spear poised, waiting for a sign.

CHARLES WRIGHT, JOSEPHINE JACOBSEN AND ELLEN BRYANT VOIGT

Why is most contemporary poetry so dull?

Consider three thoughts that occurred to me while reading the work of Charles Wright: his ideas are uninteresting, his poems undramatic; his language is only intermittently charged or lyrical; he is among the best-known poets of his generation. If you believe, as I do, that these three statements do not add up, you will also catch the drift of my rhetorical opening. We live in a world in which reputation has little to do with accomplishment. Given the broad context of contemporary American poetry, often so prosaic and self-regarding that it turns away anyone who is not a "professional reader," Charles Wright is a relatively honorable practitioner. Yet, going over most of his work in preparation to review *Chickamauga*, his new collection, I found very little that would justify paying hard-earned money to acquire it. Most of his poems are so flat and passive that they should have been left in a drawer; instead, they have been published in prominent magazines like *The New Yorker*.

Wright's defenders will remind you of his Italian and Oriental influences, his long apprenticeship to Pound's *Cantos*, etc. Some will also tell you that Wright's project is now to thwart the reader's expectations, as if the reader were merely an inconvenience. Reviewing *Chickamauga* in *The New Republic* (August 7, 1995), Helen

Vendler performed extraordinary verbal gymnastics (and ultimately made a fool of herself), trying to prove Wright a major poet. Of his title poem, she writes, "[It] climbs to a vantage point where the anonymity of history has blanked out the details." History without details? What a brilliant idea! While we're at it, how about poetry without words? How about humming a few bars on a kazoo and calling it an epic? Vendler has often been a very good critic, and she should know better; she even extols Wright as a poet without qualities: "No objects, then; and no self, and no God. Has there ever been a more stringent set of requirements for poetry?" Never a duller one, I'll wager.

Slightly later, Professor Vendler anticipates my objections: "Such a poem will not be your choice if you are set on lyric that maintains the illusion of a direct mimetic personal speech by 'suppressing' its status as composed and measured language." But I still don't follow her; is she really suggesting that direct and personal lyrics suppress their status as measured language? Doesn't she remember her own work on Keats and Yeats? Weren't those poets both personal and measured? She calls Wright "interesting" because he is "a poet who wants to acknowledge in each of his poems that a poem is a coded piece of language and yet wants also to express, by that very code, the certainty that a piece of language exhibiting structure, grammar and syntax is not 'found art,' but has been arranged by a questing human consciousness forever incommunicado beneath its achieved mask." Read that passage again, then claw the wool from your eyes and you will see that Professor Vendler is either committing fraud or has lost her grip. She uses words like "measured language" and "structure," but never satisfactorily explains how they pertain to the poetry at hand. The insufficiency of art has been a subject of lyric poetry for a very long time, but never before the twentieth century has that subject been used to justify such complacency.

Meanwhile, what about poor Charles Wright? Wade through his watery oeuvre, and you will find moments of real precision. In one early poem, he remarks, "The evening, like / An old dog, circles the hills, / Anxious to settle." It's a fine, lovingly Southern image. But in the same book, *The Grave of the Right Hand*, one finds Wright at his weakest: "I would say, off-hand, that things / Are beginning to happen... ." His well-known poem "Two Stories," from *The Other Side of the River* concludes, "I'm starting to think about the psychotransference of all things." These quotations are wrenched out of contexts that are not much more poetic. Wright's weaker poems require a too-generous, tone-deaf critic like Vendler to give them stature, and many unsuspecting readers may not comprehend the power Vendler wields in the world of poetry, despite her questionable taste.

There is plenty of meditative near-spirituality in *Chickamauga*, but it's all air and light, history without the details:

> If sentences constitute
>
>   everything we believe,
>
> Vocabularies retool
> Our inability to measure and get it right,
> And languages don't exist.
> That's one theory. Here's another:
> Something weighs on our shoulders
> And settles itself like black light
>
>   invisibly in our
>
>   hair...

Since critics don't buy the books they review, they have the luxury of praising hogwash. Pity the reader who gets suckered into paying for it. Wright disappoints me because he can at times create a lovely, rich lyricism, as in a poem with a clumsy title, "After Reading Tu Fu, I Go Outside to the Dwarf Orchard," but his asceticism and habitual prosiness betray the very strengths he should be building on. He can do better, though in the present context he has precious little reason to try.

Josephine Jacobsen, on the other hand, has been trying hard all her long life; her new collection charts both her restlessness and her achievement. While Charles Wright's work takes on a formal and intellectual uniformity that becomes fruitlessly repetitive, Ms. Jacobsen has never fallen into such a rut. Born in Canada in 1908, but long a citizen of this country, she has flirted with several modern literary trends—including surrealism and the sort of linguistic diffidence we see in Wright—without ever losing her head to them. By remaining a maker, she rescues her poems from self-parody; she understands the material value of verse, free or measured. Frequently compared to Marianne Moore and Elizabeth Bishop, she shares their reticence and fascination with detail. She especially resembles Bishop in her love of travel; the peripatetic muse has inspired many of her best poems. But her poems would not be so charming if Ms. Jacobsen did not first learn how to make charm happen, as she does in this early poem, "Spring, Says the Child":

There are words too ancient to be said by the lips of a child—
Too old, too old for a child's soft reckoning—
Ancient, terrible words, to a race unreconciled:
Death, spring...

The composite heart of man knows their awful age—
They are frightening words to hear on a child's quick tongue.
They overshadow, with their centuries' heritage,
The tenderly young.
Death, says the child, *spring*, says the child, and *heaven* ...
This is flesh against stone, warm hope against salt sea—
This is all things soft, young, ignorant; this is even
Mortality.

Charm is the surface beauty that lures us into the soul of poetry; it is precisely the quality most contemporary poetry lacks. In contrast to Wright's *Chickamauga,* Jacobsen's *In the Crevice of Time* is worth buying and going back to; we are called to the poems by their precision, their formal affirmations—even though the world they depict trembles with uncertainty. This is not to say there are no flawed pieces in the book; on many occasions she cripples rhythm or adopts language too fragmentary or opaque to matter. I prefer her when she is deliberately commanding. I also find her attitude toward art and life humane, as in the following lines about a prehistoric cave painter:

Our hulking confrère scraping the wall,
piling the dust over the motionless face:
in the abyss of time how he is close,
his art an act of faith, his grave
an act of art: for all, for all,
a celebration and a burial.

I could go on, listing her triumphs in poems like "Birdsong of the Lesser Poet," "Gentle Reader," "An Absence of Slaves," "Pondicherry Blues," "Mr. Mahoney," "The Provider," "The Sisters," "The Birthday Party" and "Survivor's Ballad," but there is no space here to do justice to a poet who has done such justice to us.

Giving the world its due—that is a fine task for the poet, not succumbing to some easy and self-defeating relativism. As a reader I appreciate poets who command the page and, better still, the voice. Precise and memorable language arises from such control, and the greatest poets take our breath away by writing nearly always at that pitch. No one considered in this review comes up to that level—Shakespeare has not been reincarnated—but in the best of the twenty-nine books I considered, there were glimmerings of hope for the language, which in turn gave me hope about life. That is a paradox of poetry; it can sing despairingly and find help in the song. It can also tell stories. Both singing and storytelling are poetry's most ancient and enduring functions, and I find it incredible that so many contemporary poets attempt to deny this truth one way or another.

Luckily, we have good writers like Ellen Bryant Voigt who give us sturdy, lucid poems. In her new book, *Kyrie*, Voigt creates a polyphonic narrative about the influenza pandemic in the aftermath of WW I. Given the magnitude of her topic—twenty-five million deaths worldwide, half a million in the U.S. alone—I am surprised to recall having read so little about it before now. These statistics demonstrate that in approximately one year, 1918-19, we lost nearly as many Americans as were killed in the entire Civil War, and the occurrence of new viral strains reminds us that the disaster Voigt recounts could happen again.

The plague and AIDS have made huge impressions upon literature; perhaps influenza seems too common by comparison, less dramatic. In any case, Voigt makes an involving book out of it. Written as a sequence of short poems, some of them sonnets and what you might call pseudo-sonnets, *Kyrie* resembles a smaller *Spoon River Anthology* in its assembly of voices. But Voigt does not name many of her speakers, leaving their speech disembodied, ghostly even when they are still alive. Her short "Prologue" views the catastrophe from a distance:

After the first year, weeds and scrub;
after five, juniper and birch,
alders filling in among the briars;
ten more years, the birches crowded out,
a new world swarms on the floor of the hardwood forest.
And who can tell us where there was an orchard,
where a swing, where the smokehouse stood?

This is history with the details restored. We encounter a young woman named Mattie, witness much of the arbitrary dying through her eyes. At other points a doctor talks, or a soldier overseas who is baffled by the suffering at home. At still other points Voigt seems to search for the voice of history itself:

O, O, the world wouldn't stop—
the neighborhood grocer, the neighborhood cop
laid them down and never did rise.
And some of their children, and some of their wives,
fell into bed and never got up,
fell into bed and never got up.

This small book incorporates the long and the short views, individual suffering weighed with compassion and released to the all-encompassing tides of nature. Voigt manages a vision that is both scientific and spiritual, and in doing so she gives the world some of its due.

DANIEL MARK EPSTEIN

Some poets appear to have emerged fully formed, like Athena from the head of Zeus, but most spend years learning their craft in public, book by book. So it is not unusual to see Daniel Mark Epstein coming into his strength as he publishes his sixth volume of verse, *The Boy In the Well* (he has also published plays, prose, and works of translation). Distinguished by the Prix de Rome from the

Academy and Institute of Arts and Letters, Epstein's career was already an accomplished one before this, his finest book to date. He has been prolific, informally formal in poems ranging widely among personal and intellectual matters, nearly always lucid, occasionally visionary—though apparently, and thankfully, without any systematizing impulse.

Epstein's strong suit has always been the narrative mode, which matches his rich, ironic view of life. To my mind, he achieved a breakthrough in 1978 with the title poem of *Young Men's Gold*, a dramatic monologue of great sweep and momentum and perhaps some of the excess of Jeffers. The poem takes place in 1918, as a Civil War veteran recounts his own memories—part allegory, part folk-tale—to his grandson, "who is en route to join allied forces in France." As it happens, I have also written a long poem in which a Civil War veteran speaks as an old man in 1918, but I hadn't read Epstein's work when I conceived of mine, and I envy him some of his vivid passages. "Young Men's Gold" seems to me as stirring and disturbing as almost any narrative poem to have appeared in this country since Jeffers and Frost passed on. I say this while at the same time feeling qualms, misgivings. The poem flirts with meter and betrays it so often that its aural vitality seems compromised by indecision. Perhaps Epstein intended to let Eliot's "ghost of meter" haunt his poem. But the product, as I also find in most of Epstein's lyric output to date, sometimes lacks that jewel-cutter's precision which commands attention in whatever form.

If successful narrative poems somehow transcend their formal lapses by giving us a compromise between novelist and singer, shorter lyrics require exactitude, the greatest measure of verbal alertness. Too often Epstein's early work verged on prose, and some of those faults linger in the new book. But *The Boy in the Well* also contains some of the finest lyric and dramatic poems he has ever done. For its intellectual breadth and the technical polish of its best poems, this new collection merits high praise. In fact, though I have not thought of Epstein as a lyric poet in the past, this new volume's final poem proves me wrong; fittingly, "Helen" is a dramatic lyric, its humor both wry and knowing:

> "Tell us a love story,"
> Pleaded the class in chorus.
> "Our lessons are all done,
> Now don't lecture or bore us,"

They prattled, except for one,
Helen, whose gaze looked lost
In the maze of willow branches,
The girl the boys liked most

For the faraway blue of her eyes
and brown hair straight as rain.
"Tell us a love story, please,"
They begged the teacher again.

He frowned and longed for the bell,
Saying "All the love stories I know
End in heartache, or death—"
Then Helen, from the back row

Called at last from her daydream
In the voice of an innocent lover,
"Tell us a love story anyway
And stop before it's over."

Epstein's best lyrics all have this dramatic lucidity, with well-managed meters and stanzas that are appropriate rather than arbitrary or accidental.

The book's few apparently personal poems, such as "Lost Owl," "Book of Matches," and "Epiphany," consider the loss of safety in a dissolving family structure. But Epstein has also been adept at probing history and mythology for their psychological implications, something he manages very well in "The Ferryman," "The Hanging Gardens," and "Solomon and the Four Winds." The title poem of *The Boy in the Well* sees beyond its newspaper headline origins by imagining the altered perspective of the lost child, his distance from the continuation of life; in a sense, he has already begun that crossing with direct eyes to death's dream kingdom:

Down in the well the boy thinks he hears a cicada
Or maybe it's the strange echo of his voice.
How brightly the stars shine beyond the day
Which by now has journeyed far beyond morning.
He wishes on one star with all his might,

That Orion might reach down and save him
Or wake him from this nightmare in his own bed.
He doesn't know any more if it's day or night.
By now the children have come home from school,
All but the bravest. His mother will miss him.

Where I have reservations about Epstein's poems, I notice one of two problems: either the drama seems unfocused or opaque, or the verse loses confidence. There are passages in which Epstein teases the ear into certain aural expectations but fails to follow through. For example, here are the opening lines of "At Poe's Grave, Westminster Church," which also open the collection:

Lovers tread lightly the April grass,
Whisper among tombs, in honor and fear

Of the very souls that might bless
Their passage. This green island

Necropolis in the urban sea
Invites lovers to stroll,

Embrace out of sight of all
But the gentle dead who cannot

Hide their delight, but spin it out
In myrtle, sudden violets, wild thyme.

In the first two lines I hear four confident stresses per line, and the off-rhyme of lines one and three causes me to expect a pattern. By the time I reach "thyme" at the end of the sentence, I realize that free verse was intended — a choice that should have been apparent earlier on. There are more questions. Why is this poem in couplets? Why are lines four and five enjambed? This apparent arbitrariness in a poem that first hinted of deliberation makes me lose confidence in the writer. I found Epstein's technique more commanding in the next poem, the charmingly philosophical "After Reading 'La Demon De L'Analogy.'"

The technical traps Epstein sometimes falls into are common to our contemporaries: assigning a stanza length and then not milking it for all it's worth, assuming that enjambments needn't carry any particular significance — these lapses edge the art closer to prose. Other poems, like "Russian Village Suite" and "Jacob at Peniel," require the fuller contexts of painting or music to come fully alive. Of the former, only the final section stands freely apart from the Chagall paintings it describes, while the latter poem is the text for a ballet and has special limitations on the printed page.

Epstein is at his best, perhaps, in a dramatic monologue like "Solomon and the Four Winds" in which the wise man's son, Rehoboam, recalls his father:

> Legends feed on legends, lies on lies,
> And most of what you hear about my father
> Belongs in a book of tales of fantasies,
> Truth seen cockeyed, gossip unfit
> For scribes to copy in the sight of God.
>
> I would not give one line for your Chronicle
> Except for a certain look about your eyes
> That tells me you might write what I recall,
> No more or less....

The poem moves immediately into a story of lovely simplicity and symmetry, of wisdom balancing the chaos and trouble of our lives, and its modulated verse often captures that sense of poise, that grace which many of us seek in a work of art.

THE NEW FORMALISM
AND THE AUDIENCE FOR POETRY

All poetry is experimental poetry.
> —Wallace Stevens

No art form can be exclusively defined outside the context of its social function. Poetry has usually been a memorable utterance, an incantation or a story—all of which imply some sort of disclosure or appeal. Yet by the 1970s, many American commentators wondered whether poetry still had a significant role to play in contemporary life, and some poets were writing as if the battle for readers had already been lost. Wendell Berry's important essay, "The Specialization of Poetry," appearing in *The Hudson Review* in 1975, observed poetry's shrinking influence, which seemed to be happening despite the openly political nature of many contemporary poems. Berry was particularly incensed that interviews with poets had replaced critical essays in which poets might attempt to explain their art to a larger reading public.

Interviews can be entirely too solipsistic or egotistical; they rarely demand that poets connect their work to anything larger than a moment's whims. As Berry noted, "poets have very nearly become their own audience." This idea was to be echoed and debated in the subsequent decades, and it is of central importance to the poetic stance of the so-called New Formalists, the younger generation of American poets who have *helped* bring meter, rhyme and narrative back to American poetry.

Perhaps Berry's most important point was that poets had, in the name of freedom from traditional constraints, actually narrowed the technical range and social function of their art. He saw poets dismissing out of hand anything that smacked of tradition, like adolescents rejecting the institutions of their parents, and he accurately described the results of such ill-considered rebellion:

> That so accomplished a poet as Galway Kinnell now speaks of the suppression of narrative as a goal is, it seems to me, a serious matter, especially as it is only the latest in a series of programs to renew or purify poetry by reducing its means. Why is it necessary for poets to believe, like salesmen, that the new inevitably must replace or de-

stroy the old? Why cannot poetry renew itself and advance into new circumstance by *adding* the new to the old? Why cannot the critical faculty, in poets and critics alike, undertake to see that *the best* of the new is grafted to *the best* of the old?Free verse, for instance, is a diminishment of the competence of poetry if it is seen as *replacing* traditional prosody; it is an enlargement only if it is conceived as an addition. Freedom from narrative is a diminishment—not even a freedom—unless it is included with the capability of narrative among the live possibilities of poetry.

Berry could well have spoken for a great many younger poets coming of age at that time, poets who were sick to death of what seemed self-indulgent in the Beats and Confessional Poets, or of the excessively theoretical elements of the surrealists, the Black Mountain Poets and the New York School. To this younger generation, poetry was losing its readers at least in part because it denied its own nature, including the pleasures inherent in such techniques as meter and rhyme. Poetry that was incomprehensible or deliberately homely or self-obsessed would inevitably seem irrelevant to the reading public.

My description of these tendencies oversimplifies them, and I sidestep the question of whether free verse poets in the 1960s and 70s created any durable masterpieces. I am also aware of the many American poets of an older generation who kept meter and rhyme alive as poetic possibilities throughout this period: J.V. Cunningham, Richard Wilbur, Anthony Hecht, X.J. Kennedy, Howard Nemerov, Mona Van Duyn, John Frederick Nims, James Merrill and Donald Justice, to name a few. For the purposes of this essay, it is important to note that younger poets were often discouraged from using rhyme and meter, except those who were fortunate enough to have the poets listed above as teachers. These young writers, and others who did not have such teachers, instinctively felt that techniques common to popular music needn't be lost to literature.

The New Formalists—poets as varied as Dana Gioia, R.S. Gwynn, Charles Martin, Timothy Steele, and Raphael Campo—have participated not only in the birth of a movement, but also in its self-description. They have consistently maintained a role in that self-description for the educated common reader, not merely for the academic specialist or the practicing poet. Broadly speaking, the last decade or so has seen a resurgence of interest in poetry throughout America, and the New Formalists may very well be on the margins of this phenomenon—they are ignored, for example, by most television programs devoted to poetry, where the old self-indulgence and pop psychology of figures like Robert Bly still prevail. Yet it appears that the New Formalists, by espousing beauty, memorability and clarity in their poems, and also by embracing the complex subject matter of their generation, may in fact represent trends of larger cultural relevance. The movement has become a subject of conferences and academic papers, and, much more importantly, it has brought new vigor to poetic qualities many readers assumed were lost to younger generations. In America, one continually meets people who quit reading poetry because it no longer gave them pleasure, people who assumed that the ancient idea of the poet as a maker with some social role to play had entirely died out.

However, if the term "New Formalist" is a self-description adopted by a growing number of American poets, it is also a very strange one; it began as a term of derision and dismissal in attacks launched by the movement's antagonists. Essays written by Ariel Dawson, Diane Wakoski, Ira Sadoff, Wayne Dodd and others dismissed New Formalists as Reaganite conservatives, as anglophile sentimentalists, as socially moribund aesthetes. A recent review by Philip Dacey referred to them as "bean-counters making extravagant gestures."

Formalist poets have, in fact, come from virtually every class and quarter of American society: every race, every sexual and political persuasion. There are no limits to the subjects they might write about, from Lesbian love in the poems of Marilyn Hacker, to libraries, farms and family life in those of Timothy Steele; from R.S. Gwynn's tender spirituality in "Release" to his sadness over Viet Nam in "Body Bags" to his several satires of commercial culture. This list could go on; suffice it to say that the New Formalists (or "the Few Normalists," as Gwynn once quipped) cannot be categorized by politics or gender, only by generation and the diversity of their subjects and forms.

The movement arose in the 1970s, but took at least a decade to gain momentum. In his preface to a tiny anthology called *Shaping*

(Dryad Press, 1978), Philip K. Jason wrote, "We are now witnessing a reaction against decades of poetry that has tried to do more with less: less sonic density, less rhythmic backbone, less line integrity—less of almost all of those conventions by which poetry had distinguished itself from other literary genres." Yet there was no consensus among literary critics—at least the few critics who still read poetry as anything but a vehicle for political discourse—that meter could reclaim a significant role in American poetry. As the critic Robert McPhillips has noted, first books by Charles Martin and Timothy Steele, published in 1978 and 1979 respectively, went nearly unnoticed.

Martin's *Room for Error* exhibits not only the classical poise of a poet who would later become one of our best translators of Catullus, but a refreshing willingness to find his subjects in popular culture, as he does in "Taken Up":

> Tired of earth, they dwindled on their hill,
> Watching and waiting in the moonlight until
> The aspens' leaves quite suddenly grew still,
>
> No longer quaking as the disc descended,
> That glowing wheel of lights whose coming ended
> All waiting and watching. When it landed
>
> The ones within it one by one came forth,
> Stalking out awkwardly upon the earth,
> And those who watched them were confirmed in faith:
>
> Mysterious voyagers from outer space,
> Attenuated, golden—shreds of lace
> Spun into seeds of the sunflower's spinning face—
>
> Light was their speech, spanning mind to mind:
> We come here not believing what we find—
> Can it be your desire to leave behind
>
> The earth, which even those called angels bless,
> Exchanging amplitude for emptiness?
> And in a single voice they answered *Yes*.

Discord of human melodies all bent
To the unearthly strain of their ascent.
Come then, the strangers said, and those who were taken went.

One can compare this poem thematically to Robert Frost's "Birches"—that love of the earth we sometimes want to leave—and to Richard Wilbur's "Love Calls Us to the Things of this World," but Martin owes his imagery to the movies and the popular imagination.

Timothy Steele's work exhibits the lyric precision associated with Yvor Winters and J.V. Cunningham—the latter was Steele's teacher at Brandeis. From the start, Steele proved adept at small forms like the epigram. But he has also been able to extend his range in poems that balance logic and lyricism. He published his second collection, *Sapphics Against Anger*, with a major commercial house, and the book sold well enough to go into four printings. Its poems dealt with subjects as various as Martin Luther, L.A. traffic, and the particular affection found in his lovely "Aubade":

As she is showering, I wake to see
A shine of earrings on the bedside stand,
A single yellow sheet which, over me,
Has folds as intricate as drapery
In paintings from some fine old master's hand.

The pillow which, in dozing, I embraced
Retains the salty sweetness of her skin;
I sense her smooth back, buttocks, belly, waist,
The leggy warmth which spread and gently laced
Around my legs and loins, and drew me in.

I stretch and curl about a bit and hear her
Singing away the water's hiss and race.
Gradually the early light makes clearer
The perfume bottles by the dresser mirror,
The silver flashlight, standing on its face,

Which shares the corner of the dresser with
An ivy spilling tendrils from a cup.
And so content am I, I can forgive

Pleasure for being brief and fugitive.
I'll stretch some more, but postpone getting up

Until she finishes her shower and dries
(Now this and now that foot placed on a chair)
Her fine-boned ankles, and her calves and thighs,
The pink full nipples of her breasts, and ties
Her towel up, turban-style, about her hair.

This work is almost obsessively sane, and provides a real contrast to the romanticism of much American poetry. Steele's first two books have been reprinted by the University of Arkansas Press, which has also published his scholarly treatise, *Missing Measures: Modern Poetry and the Revolt Against Meter.* His third collection, *The Color Wheel,* is out from Johns Hopkins, which also publishes Charles Martin, Emily Grosholz, Tom Disch, and other New Formalist poets.

One can find quite different approaches to form and subject in the poetry of Molly Peacock and Marilyn Hacker, both of whom use rhyme and meter to liberate intimate confessions. The typical Peacock poem is identifiable less by meter than by rhyme and off-rhyme. A case in point is "Have You Ever Faked an Orgasm?" from her third collection, *Original Love:*

When I get nervous, it's hard not to.
When I'm expected to come in something
other than the ordinary way, to
take pleasure in the new way, lost, not knowing

how to drive it back to sureness...where are
the thousand thousand flowers I always pass,
the violet flannel, then the sharpness?
I can't, I can't...extinguish the star

in a burst. It goes on glowing. Your head
between my legs so long. Do you really
want to be there? I whimper as though...
then get mad. I could smash your valiant head.

"You didn't come, did you?" Naturally, you know.
Although I try to lie, the truth escapes me
almost like an orgasm itself. Then the "No"
that should crack a world, but doesn't, slips free.

Peacock is barely formal here, perhaps more interested in catching a psychological state than in maximizing verbal effects. Her rhyming words, which rarely take on special significance, act as the faintest reminders of her formal intentions.

Hacker, who must be one of the most prolific of contemporary poets, writes a kind of elevated *vers de société* in which, it seems, every aspect of her life and political opinions is chronicled. Her facility with fixed forms like sonnets, villanelles and sapphics is admirable, though I must confess that few of her poems seem sterling examples of the forms they attempt; rather, the forms are often understood, somewhat like Peacock's, to be vehicles of informality. Her best poem in sapphics is called "Elevens":

James A. Wright, my difficult older brother,
I'm in an airplane over your Ohio.
Twice a week, there and back, I make this journey
to Cincinnati.

You are six books I own and two I borrowed.
I'm the songs about the drunk on the runway,
and leaving your lover for the airport, first
thing in the morning.

You were fifty-two when you died of cancer
of the tongue, apologist for the lovely
girls who were happened to near some bleak water.
Tell me about it.

When my father died young, my mother lost it.
I am only three years younger than he was.
The older brother and the younger brother
that I never had

died young, in foreign cities, uncomforted.
Does anybody not die uncomforted?
My friend Sonny had her lovers around her
and she died also.

Half drunk on sunlight in my second country,
I yearned through six-line stanzas I learned from you.
You spent January of your last winter
up on that mountain.

I love a boy who died and a girl who left.
I love a brother who is a grown woman.
I love your eight books. I hate the ending.
I never knew you.

You knew a lot about airports and rivers
and a girl who went away in October.
Fathers, brothers and sisters die of cancer:
still, we are strangers.

You are the lonely gathering of rivers
below the plane that left you in Ohio;
you are the fog of language on Manhattan
where it's descending.

Another woman associated with the movement, Suzanne J. Doyle, has published very little, but her finest poems achieve a more impressive balance of form and content than Peacock and Hacker have so far managed. Here, from Annie Finch's anthology, *A Formal Feeling Comes*, is Doyle's poem "Hell to Pay":

When the children are asleep and our old bed
Fills with the drama of your dreams, I head
Downstairs to double check the locks and pour
Neat bourbon down, just like I did before
I ever locked a door, back when I blazed by night
Through danger in a yellow whiskey light.

I am again the wildhearted and lonely,
To whom the angel will appear, the only
Angel I have known, who drags her wings
On dance hall floors while some bright jukebox sings
Of sadness gone too sweet, and I am caught
Up in the arms of all the feeling I have fought.
Against that torn mouth no kiss comes to bless,
I answer to the shame I can't confess,
The old wound coiled up bitterly in me,
The one your love relieves but cannot free.
Hers is the power of darkness, fierce, defiled,
To which fate led me as a willing child,
And though I kneel to love to serve each day,
I know in time there will be hell to pay.

I am not sure the personal ramifications of this poem are entirely clear, but I find its subtle anxieties, its command of language and line unforgettable.

For the most part, then, these poets eschew the opacity and fragmentation of much modern art. Excessive literary allusion, poems written only for a literary or academic audience — these are qualities the New Formalists tend to avoid. But their particular brand of populism differs from that of the Beats because they believe in the viability of meter; they do not deny the value of training in traditional techniques. As esoteric, even ugly, as the term "New Formalism" sounds, most of these poets would love to be known to the widest possible readership, and many have explicitly argued for the rediscovery of this popular audience. No one has done so more passionately and elegantly than Dana Gioia, whose critical book, *Can Poetry Matter?*, has received international notice. Gioia has been dismissed as often as he has been praised, but in my view he is an important literary figure. His two collections of poems, *Daily Horoscope* and *The Gods of Winter*, have in some ways fared better in England, where their poise and complex emotions have found appreciative readers. But his books have also done well in the States, and I suspect that fact alone has caused some lesser talents to stand jealously against him.

Unlike some of the poets quoted so far, Gioia occasionally writes free verse, as in one of his most beautiful poems, "Planting a Sequoia." Though he is good at rhyme and sometimes chooses fixed forms like the triolet and the sestina, much of his best work, including several superb narrative poems, is in blank verse. There are those who, forgetting the example of Tennyson's "Tears, Idle Tears," hold that blank verse cannot be a successful vehicle of lyric poetry. Gioia's new poem, "Metamorphosis," proves them wrong; it is also a superb example of literary allusion driven by emotional necessity:

> There were a few, the old ones promised us,
> Who could escape. A few who once, when trapped
> At the extreme of violence, reached out
> Beyond the rapist's hand or sudden blade.
>
> Their fingers branched and blossomed. Or they leapt
> Unthinking from the heavy earth to fly
> With voices—ever softer—that became
> The admonitions of the nightingale.
>
> They proved, like cornered Daphne twisting free,
> There were a few whom even the great gods
> Could not destroy.
>   And you, my gentle ghost,
> Did you break free before the cold hand clutched?
> Did you escape into the lucid air
> Or burrow secretly among the dark
> Expectant roots, to rise again with them
> As the unknown companion of the spring?
>
> I'll never know, my changeling, where you've gone,
> And so I'll praise you—flower, bird, and tree—
> My nightingale awake among the thorns,
> My laurel tree that marks a god's defeat,
> My blossom bending on the water's edge,
> Forever lost within your inward gaze.

Fine individual poems have a way of dwarfing all concern for the shape and well-being of a movement, and I believe the last six lines of "Metamorphosis" to be among the loveliest written in English in recent decades.

While Gioia is well-known, largely due to his textbooks, his criticism and translations from several languages, R.S. Gwynn is still too little known even in America. His first book, *The Drive-In*, was one of the best single volumes produced by anyone associated with the movement, but it is now out of print. Gwynn has published two superb chapbook-length collections, *Body Bags* and *The Area Code of God*, as well as an hilarious literary satire, *The Narcissiad*; those who love his work, as I do, eagerly await another full-length collection. He has written humorous songs, like "The Professor's Lot" (modeled on Gilbert and Sullivan) and poems that seem intended for English majors, like the splendid tour de force "Approaching a Significant Birthday, He Peruses *The Norton Anthology of Poetry*." But Gwynn's finest poems rise above such genre considerations to a near-visionary pitch, as if the poet-as-prophet faced God from the sturdiest formal scaffolding. For the sake of brevity, I will quote his quietest poem, and one of the two best examples we have of the curtal sonnet (the other being Hopkins'). It is "Release," a poem I mentioned earlier:

> Slow for the sake of flowers as they turn
>   Toward sunlight, graceful as a line of sail
>   Coming into the wind. Slow for the mill-
> Wheel's heft and plummet, for the chug and churn
>   Of water as it gathers, for the frail
>   Half-life of spraylets as they toss and spill.
>
> For all that lags and eases, all that shows
>   The winding-downward and diminished scale
>   Of days declining to a twilit chill,
> Breathe quietly, release into repose:
>   Be still.

This is serious in the best sense of the word, but Gwynn is also one of our finest authors of comic verse. There are other good humorists among the New Formalists. One thinks of Gail White, of Jack Butler's "Attack of the Zombie Poets," and of many poems by Tom Disch, including "Ballade of the New God":

I have decided I'm divine.
Caligula and Nero knew
A godliness akin to mine,
But they are strictly hitherto.
They're dead, and what can dead gods do?
I'm here and now. I'm dynamite.
I'd worship me if I were you.
A new religion starts tonight!

No booze, no pot, no sex, no swine:
I have decreed them all taboo.
My words will be your only wine,
The thought of me your honey dew.
All other thoughts you will eschew.
You'll call yourself a Thomasite
And hymn my praise with loud yahoo.
A new religion starts tonight.

But (you might think) that's asinine!
I'm just as much a god as you.
You may have built yourself a shrine,
But I won't bend my knee. Who
Asked you to be my god? I do,
Who am, as god, divinely right.
Now you must join my retinue:
A new religion starts tonight.

All that I have said is true.
I'm god, and you're my acolyte.
Surrender's bliss. I envy you.
A new religion starts tonight.

Disch has been for some years a well-known novelist, which
raises the related phenomenon of the New Narrative in poetry. If
the resurgence of meter and rhyme suggests kinds of pleasure that
poetry readers have too often been denied, a similar concept of
audience, of art that communicates in memorable terms, applies to

narrative forms. Such work is largely beyond the scope of this essay, but I do want to mention a few poets associated with the New Narrative. Frederick Turner has published two science fiction epics in verse: *The New World* and *Genesis*; Vikram Seth has also done a novel in elaborately-rhymed stanzas, *The Golden Gate* (Seth is from India, but was partly educated at Stanford University, where he knew Timothy Steele and other New Formalist poets). Robert McDowell and Mark Jarman have both published book-length narrative poems. Jarman's *Iris* is in a free-verse line adapted from Robinson Jeffers, while McDowell's *The Diviners* is in blank verse. Another narrative poet, Andrew Hudgins, has done a book-length sequence, *After the Lost War*, and many shorter narratives, often quite funny, based upon his family history. Narrative is inherently social, and verse techniques borrowed from past masters like Milton, Pushkin, Robinson, Frost and Jeffers remain in use, extending the range of the possible for contemporary poetry.

In the long run, however, no poet could be entirely happy to find that he or she is hemmed in with a herd, even an attractive one. Poets are individuals; they swim in schools only part of the time, and I should at least mention several more of these individuals: Timothy Murphy, a superb lyric poet who also happens to be a venture capitalist living in North Dakota; Mary Jo Salter and Brad Leithauser, who form another sort of partnership, managing their successful writing careers from Massachusetts; Dick Davis, a brilliant English poet and translator who lives and teaches in Ohio; Greg Williamson, whose first book, *The Silent Partner*, made one of the best debuts in recent decades, and Suzanne Noguere, who waited years to publish her fine first book, *Whirling Round the Sun*.

I have tried here to describe the outlines of the movement, and to nominate some of its ablest practitioners. But ultimately our judgment of any poet has to do with the question of whether or not that poet has produced masterpieces of the art. If I have high hopes for *some* New Formalists, I should also admit that the majority of poets associated with the movement are as mediocre as poets in any other group. The finest of the New Formalists try to bring neglected resources of the English language to bear on contemporary experience; their work needn't be explained away by theorists, but can be read by anyone interested in poetry. We must, as Wendell Berry suggested, find what is *best* in the new and the old. I have added that the best ought to speak to readers as people, not only as specialists. This idea of audience, much older than Wordsworth's emphasis of it in his Preface, has been forgotten by too many critics writing now. The aim of these new poets is song, to paraphrase Frost, or passionate normal speech, as Yeats put it. They are of that tradition, even as they try to make it new. Any judgments we make of them, as a group or as individuals, are necessarily preliminary. Time, the toughest arbiter of all, will have the last word.

There are very few contemporary critics of poetry whose essays and reviews make essential reading, but Dana Gioia is one of them. Writing in *The Hudson Review*, *The Atlantic*, *The Nation*, *Verse*, and other magazines large and small, Gioia has presented his views in essays that are beautiful for their classical poise and lucidity. Now that he has collected twenty-three of them in his first critical book, *Can Poetry Matter?* (Graywolf Press), it is possible to see yet another of Gioia's virtues: his compelling vision of poetry's place in contemporary culture as an embattled but still viable art. "I wrote these essays with the conviction that poetry appeals to a broader audience than is usually acknowledged," he tells us in his Preface. That conviction, found throughout the book, is the basis for its fundamental coherence and importance.

One has only to read other contemporary critics to realize that Gioia's conviction is not universally shared. J.D. McClatchy's 1989 *White Paper*, for example, argues,

> That day is gone when the reader, taking up a new poem for the first time, can comfortably dismiss it as "too difficult." Our professional readers—critics and teachers, and of course the poets themselves—have accustomed us to respect the authority of difficulty, and no longer as a mere problem, but as a necessary condition of true poetry, and of our theories about it.

McClatchy assumes a small, professional readership that will be receptive to his subsequent ideas about poets who are already securely canonized.

Contrast this with Gioia's opening sentences:

> I have read poetry as long as I have been able to read. Before that, my mother, a woman of no advanced education, read or recited it to me from memory. Consequently, I have never considered poetry an intrinsically difficult art whose mysteries can be appreciated only by a trained elite. Poetry is an art—like painting or jazz, opera or drama—whose pleasures are generally open to any intelligent person with the inclination to savor them.

Gioia's assumptions allow him to appreciate poets who are often undervalued in the academy, and to confront beliefs that have relegated contemporary poetry to what he calls a "subculture."

Nearly two generations ago, Randall Jarrell complained that "poems, stories, new-made works of art, are coming to seem rather less congenial and important than they once did, both to literary and not-so-literary readers." He could have been writing last week. Our nation now produces too many graduate students and teachers who would rather eat shoe leather than read poetry, so they cannot or will not convey its pleasures to other readers. Gioia's careful response to Jarrell's complaint may not cure the disease, but his diagnosis is one we very much need to hear.

He focuses the present volume on American literary life, writing three kinds of essays: overviews of culture and poetics, historical pieces designed to rescue the reputations of neglected poets, and arguments casting new light on the lives and works of poets who are well known. A good example of the first sort is the title essay, which caused quite a stir when it first appeared in *The Atlantic*.

Gioia acknowledges that poetry currently has a kind of popularity, but argues that it is limited to a narrow segment of the reading public. This popularity (its visible signs are creative writing programs, public readings and poetry journals) is found almost exclusively on college campuses. Poets have, of course, appeared on *Nightline* and at presidential inaugurations, but poetry's importance in the daily life of most educated Americans is surely questionable. Gioia worries about all those possible readers out there, the millions for whom poetry might offer something of real value, but for whom the university is not the New Jerusalem. Most critics have failed to wonder about potential non-academic audiences precisely because they are professors. I'm a professor myself, and I know how dangerously easy it is to exaggerate the importance of the classroom and its values, whatever they might be. But Gioia spent fifteen years as a business executive in a huge corporation, and his vision of American culture is less blinkered than that of many academic critics, for whom business and poetry cannot mix.

The desire to find a popular audience for poetry should not be confused with anti-intellectualism. Gioia is also astonishingly well-read in a variety of fields. I can't help delighting when he uses Marxian economics to identify the problem with the creative writing programs:

As Marx maintained and few economists have disputed, changes in a class's economic function eventually transform its values and behavior. In poetry's case, the socioeconomic changes have led to a divided literary culture: the superabundance of poetry within a small class and the impoverishment outside it. One might even say that outside the classroom—where society demands that the two groups interact—poets and the common reader are no longer on speaking terms.

The increasing professionalism of the poet-professor has clearly been healthy in economic terms; few of us are starving in garrets any more. Robert Frost was able to say, "The English department may be the poet's best and surest friend." But it has also created whole classes of poets whose strongest loyalties are to each other, not to the educated common reader. Partly this is due to the ruthless competition for teaching jobs, but in many academic circles even the notion of a common reader is openly derided as a sentimental fantasy. Poets become increasingly cynical and expedient; for example, Gioia accurately observes that several anthologies of contemporary poetry serve poets more than readers, and that poetry reviewing has lost credibility by being too kind to the work of shabby practitioners.

As an alternative to this mutual back scratching Gioia offers the poet-critics of the mid-century: Jarrell, Schwartz, Blackmur, Kees, etc. His justifiable praise of their achievements does make them seem rather more altruistic than they probably were, and he neglects the fact that some of those earlier writers also benefited from academic positions and professional favors. But his point about the neglect of nonacademic readers remains valid even with these historical simplifications. Most essays in poetics from Sidney to Bly have offered narrow readings of the past to justify their own aims. As Eliot observed, "the poet . . . is always trying to defend the kind of poetry he is writing, or to formulate the kind he wants to write." Gioia's distinction as a contemporary advocate is that he wants a broader audience to be included in the poet's plans.

Here Gioia makes his six "modest proposals" for poets, teachers and arts administrators. Though some are not so uncommon as he implies, they are all helpful reminders that poetry is more important than our own careers. For me, number five is especially urgent: *"Poetry teachers, especially at the high-school and undergraduate levels, should spend less time on analysis and more on performance."* One reason so many students turn away from poetry is that poets and teachers have focused so intently on classroom analysis. Poems known only by such conceptual means are not known at all, and seldom enjoyed. My father-in-law, a Scottish immigrant with little formal education, could recite hundreds of lines of Robert Burns and border ballads, not only because he was trained to respect them, but because they carried his language into the New World, speaking to his most powerful memories and losses. Gioia understands that we are losing such readers, as well as educated professionals in fields other than poetry, and challenges us to recall them to the art.

Some theorists would dismiss Gioia's primary assumptions about the relationship between poet and reader as philosophically naive or quixotic, but the alternatives seem to me rather bleak. Whole libraries of turgid academic prose make it abundantly clear that we ignore the common reader—or at least the belief in one—at our own peril. In "The Poet in an Age of Prose," Gioia reminds us that "The composition of a poem requires—either consciously or intuitively—the notion of an audience." Like a skillful mediator who has the reading public's interests in mind, Gioia looks for some way of speaking to the many:

> Good poetry never underestimates its readers. It actively seeks their imaginative and intellectual collaboration by assuming and exploiting a common frame of reference.

That "common frame" implies the now-heretical notion of an "available tradition," and here again Gioia exposes himself to ideological sniping; some critics would have us accept the eternal balkanization of poetry's audience. The point, however, is that we need to empathize with what seems unlike us in order to discover the kinds of experience we all share. Randall Jarrell put it this way:

> When you begin to read a poem you are entering a foreign country whose laws and language and life are a kind of translation of your own; but to accept it because its stews taste exactly like your old

mother's hash, or to reject it because the owl-headed goddess of wisdom in its temple is fatter than the Statue of Liberty, is an equal
mark of want of imagination....

In other words, we need a poetry that will help us imagine, even
through "foreign" particulars, what is universally human.

While Gioia apparently has no desire to banish all difficulty from
the art, he criticizes the solipsism of the confessional poets and the
hollowness of surrealists, two schools that share the romantic elevation of the poet. He has advocated what is sometimes derisively
called the New Formalism, and here he defends the movement despite its silly name. These poets, a varied collection, have tried to
use traditional forms as well as free verse to bring common American experience to a larger readership. Gioia speaks of their "unem-
barrassed employment of heightened popular speech, and the res-
toration of direct, unironic emotion." If all that sounds familiar from
Dryden and Wordsworth, it should; Gioia's critical stance is only
revolutionary in his willingness to attack sacred cows, but his belief in communication characterizes his own practice as a poet. I
have taught Gioia's second book of poems, *The Gods of Winter*, to
several college classes, and have been struck by its strong appeal
to my students, who frequently find Gioia's poems both accessible
and moving, even though the poems don't coddle or patronize them
as readers.

In "Notes on the New Formalism" Gioia argues that for years
we have neglected one of poetry's primary pleasures, its control of
patterned or unpatterned sounds, while placing most of our emphasis on its content. One would be foolish to divorce poetry from
ideas, and Gioia certainly advocates nothing of the sort; he simply
reminds us that verse needs to be distinguishable from prose, just
as poetry is usually distinguishable from criticism. We need variety, as he also argues in a more dated essay, "The Dilemma of the
Long Poem." It's not just variety of practice that Gioia is after, but
also variety of experience. In his wonderful article, "Business and
Poetry," he decries the publish-or-perish culture of the academy,
which so often rewards hasty work, and points out that a surprisingly large number of American poets have made a living in the
business world. Gioia himself has since left General Foods, moving with his family back to California. He admits that the long hours

and short vacations are not especially conducive to writing, but he also points out that writers outside the academy can afford to delay publication of their books until they are good, rather than rushing into print to keep a job. Furthermore, business is a major aspect of American life that is nearly absent from our poetry:

> Modern American poets have written superbly of bicycles, of ground-hogs, of laundry left out to dry, of baseball cards and telephone poles. One of Randall Jarrell's best poems depicts a supermarket. Elizabeth Bishop has written movingly about an atlas, and Robert Lowell about breaking in a pair of contact lenses. James Dickey found a way to put animals in heaven, and Ezra Pound put many of his London literary acquaintances in hell. Sodomy, incest, and pedophilia have been domesticated by our domineering national Muse as readily as have skunks, armadillos, hop toads, and at least one wart hog. But somehow this same poetic tradition has never been able to look inside the walls of a corporate office and see with the same intensity what forty million Americans do during the week.

American poetry makes democratic claims about subject matter, but it remains primarily a romantic poetry that consigns business to the realm of the unpoetic, as if money were imagination's enemy, our dirtiest family secret, instead of a universal form of communication and exchange. Our hypocrisy about money stems from the same puritanism that would deny us pleasure in verse because it is insufficiently "difficult" or "serious."

At times these essays in culture and poetics assault a perceived status quo, and for some that will remain the central weakness of Gioia's book: his reliance on "straw man" arguments to create a vulnerable enemy. Yet many of his targets are less straw than flesh and blood, hence the irritation of certain readers. Anyone who dares to be ambitious is bound to be disliked, I suppose, and Gioia adds to ambition the appalling crime of honesty. He is our necessary gadfly.

But he is also capable of generous praise, and this is best seen in three essays intended to rescue relatively neglected poets: Robinson Jeffers, Weldon Kees and Ted Kooser. In each case, Gioia depicts a critical establishment limited by its own categories and incapable of discussing poets who do not conform to them. Critics trained to explicate Eliot, Pound, Stevens or Ashbery are speechless before the once-popular narratives of Jeffers, the dark mythology of Kees or Kooser's local habitations. Gioia places each of these poets in clear historical contexts, then illuminates particular poems for the pleasure or instruction they provide. "The Loneliness of Weldon Kees" is superb literary history, its final sentences rising to an impassioned eloquence:

> Kees used the detritus of a spiritually bankrupt society—the ephemera of slang, popular songs, brand names, advertising, fashion, journalism, movies—to provide a backdrop stark enough to dramatize the human situation. He practiced a realism so bitter it borders on prophecy. He presented only the choices history offered his generation, and none of them were attractive. There are contemporary poets more modern than Kees, but none of them seems truer to modern life. He wrote about the noisy world we are trapped in, about the spoiled landscapes that surround us, using the sordid images that confront us every day. Many writers tried to fuse these fragments into art, but few had the necessary imaginative energy. Kees did. He is the poet our age deserves—whether it wants him or not.

"The Anonymity of the Regional Poet" is important not only for what it says about Kooser's quirky, intensely visual and well-wrought poems, but for its discussion of regionalism:

> One would think that after Yeats and Faulkner, Joyce and Svevo, Verga and Cather, Cavafy and Hardy, regional writing would no longer be perceived as a second-class artistry practiced by those incapable of presenting the world at large.

It is true that writers—even New York writers—are classified by locale more often than by talent. Kooser's reputation may also have suffered because of the straightforwardness of his poems, which could make academic critics feel useless, like wallflowers at a party. Helen Vendler may insist that "No art work describes itself," but readers of Kooser's best poems have little to do but nod in recognition of their accuracy. These essays show Gioia at his best, a reader of catholic tastes defending genuine artists.

When he turns to poets whose reputations are firmly established, he reminds us again how much pleasure can be derived from literary history. Essays on Stevens and Eliot add to our understanding of both poets' obsessively bourgeois lives. The Eliot essay is particularly fine, and begins on a note of high drama crucial to Gioia's reading of the poet's letters: "In June 1915, Thomas Stearns Eliot, a twenty-six-year-old American graduate student on a traveling fellowship to Oxford, committed the one rash act of his life. He married Vivien Haigh-Wood, a vivacious young Englishwoman he had met only a few months before." Eliot's first marriage was indeed a disaster in many ways, though Gioia could have said more than he does about Vivien's generous support of her husband's writing. Still, his reading of the letters is magnificent, humanizing Eliot by showing us the young man who never really escaped the disapproval of his parents or their image of the decent life. Poets have always wondered how to reconcile the demands of their art with those of life, so it is especially important that we have more than one image of the living poet—the responsible citizen as well as the romantic rebel or the hysterical suicide.

Gioia's most notorious essay, "The Successful Career of Robert Bly," is as skillful a piece of demolition as one is likely to find in contemporary criticism. When it first appeared in *The Hudson Review*, you could practically hear the spontaneous combustion of Bly's fervent followers all over the country. They were so busy blowing their tops that they failed to notice passages in which Gioia actually praises Bly (citing the anti-war poems, among others). He attacks Bly for his obsessive publicity, but most poets, including Gioia, know how necessary publicity is. Poetry makes its way into the world so slowly and quietly that every generation has needed energetic pamphleteers to give it a boost. When he writes that "Bly saw himself at odds with the literary establishment—both in the academy and in New York . . . ," Gioia could also be referring to himself. Even the reticent T.S. Eliot, as his letters prove, knew how to calculate the impact of his work. But Bly frequently couples advertisement with incompetence, both as a poet and a translator, and here Gioia's charges are leveled with withering accuracy:

> In his hands, dramatically different poets like Lorca and Rilke, Montale and Machado, not only all sounded alike, they all sounded like Robert Bly, and even then not like Bly at his best. But as if that

weren't bad enough, Bly consistently held up these diminished versions as models of poetic excellence worthy of emulation. In promoting his new poetics..., he set standards so low that he helped create a school of mediocrities largely ignorant of the premodern poetry in English and familiar with foreign poetry only through oversimplified translations.

Gioia doesn't mention Bly's very readable translation of Knut Hamsun 's novel, *Hunger*, but what he says about the verse is often painfully true.

In a later essay, "The Example of Elizabeth Bishop," he offers still more criticisms of the self-serving poets who rose to prominence in the sixties:

> When Charles Bukowski stumbled on stage carrying a six-pack of beer, the crowd would squeal with delight. They hardly cared what was said as long as he kept in character. When Robert Bly donned a pig mask and spoke in funny voices or Allen Ginsberg jingled his finger-cymbals like a Hollywood gypsy, the resulting art form often had less to do with poetry than with TV wrestling.

Not all popularity, Gioia seems to argue, is worthy of poetry. Without overpraising Bishop or other admirable poets like Donald Justice, he suggests how much more we can learn from their attentiveness to their art than from the hollow theatrics of a Bly or a Ginsberg.

Finally, the selection from his omnibus reviews provides examples of Gioia's critical stance in miniature form. He proves patient even with poets he criticizes, like Margaret Atwood, John Ashbery and the later James Dickey. When he writes that "Ashbery is a discursive poet without a subject," he has said more in one sentence than Ashbery's acolytes have managed in their volumes. The poets Gioia praises most are substantial writers who usually publish little and work patiently outside the literary limelight: Jared Carter, Theodore Weiss, Radcliffe Squires and the now better-known Tom Disch. Gioia apparently believes that the last thing we need are more essays on writers who are already famous, unless those essays really do provide new information or insight. He has the courage to cast a cold eye on what passes for the new, and to praise with real eloquence good work that has been neglected.

"I have done more omnibus reviews than I care to remember," he writes. "They require an immense amount of time. They pay miserably. And they usually attract little attention. They are, in short, the very model of poetry criticism." Plenty of contemporary poets have written criticism, but few have done it so clear-headedly. By his own lucid and thoughtful example, Gioia offers an affirmative answer to the question posed by his book's title. Of course poetry matters, poets have said all along. But in the steel-and-glass world of the corporate headquarters, the airports, the interstate truck stops, the small businesses that, for better and worse, make up so much of American life, his question is not rhetorical. I cannot know whether his ideas will continue to bear fruit, or will be neglected like some of the poets he praises here, but I can assert that Dana Gioia's criticism matters as much as any now being written.

OTHER LIVES: ON SHORTER NARRATIVE POEMS

Empathy, the act of inhabiting a stranger's experience, is a civilizing process. It implies connection, community, releasing the poet—who otherwise seems "Encased in talent like a uniform"— from isolation. Fiction's advantage has usually been considered its interest in society as well as the lives of specific individuals, and poets can envy this, particularly when the lyric "I" has become repetitious, nearly automatic. Tennyson and Browning began in Romantic subjectivity, and balanced their careers on the taut line between those early impulses and an opposing impulse toward the objectivity of storytelling. In our time the line has been stretched between similar poles; one mode of expression loses power through overuse, and poets naturally turn to the opposite mode to restore vital tension. Rather than leaping to the conclusion that the subjective lyric is dead and we can only stay aloft on the shoulders of a good story, we should admit that there are advantages and disadvantages to every genre, and that poets are better off when they can write more than one kind of poem.

Anthony Hecht and Louis Simpson have written about the use of narrative to regain literary territory that in modern times has been lost to the novel. More recently, a younger generation of poets, including Robert McDowell, Mark Jarman, and Dana Gioia, has argued that narrative may be a good way to work free of the lethargy observable in many contemporary poems. Recent uses of narrative are broader than this short list suggests, yet poets and critics have, so far, neglected fundamental questions about these practices. For example, is the poetic line as viable today for characterization as it was a century (or twenty-five centuries) ago? What are the objectives and difficulties of characterization in verse? If poets and their audience can rejoin in empathy's embrace, what sort of poem will best invite and challenge them?

There are at least two good reasons why contemporary poets might use verse to create characters and tell stories. One reason is that it can rejuvenate their art by compelling them to reevaluate the subjects they write about, to look more closely at lives usually deemed insufficiently flashy or spectacular. By involving us in the nuances of social and individual problems, narrative poetry can address issues beyond the narrow confines of the poet's life, or it can focus emotions too painfully personal to be revealed directly in a lyric. It is also possible that the line has advantages lacking in

butes to memorability, help-
us would agree is in danger
nd is tremendously impor-
t and feeling; it can contrib-
particular ways, adding an-
telling.
fullest in shorter narratives
recited in a single session.
ll-written as Vikram Seth's
derick Turner's science fic-
re, in our culture, too long
ed aural performances, and
lers over a longer period of
of several book-length po-
mbly of ghosts in *The Chang-*
's pseudo-autobiographical
Corn's *Notes from a Child of*
essed the revival of shorter
and Simpson, and younger
er, Robert McDowell, An-
ove and Dana Gioia. Like
to produce their impact by
ey can be absorbed by an

audience in their entirety, rather than in fragments or highlights. Due to their relative brevity, they cannot afford a leisurely alternation of prose-like passages and lyric moments; their lines must be more consistently commanding and intense. In shorter narratives the partnership of line and narrative structure is particularly important. We can hear the adjustments of dramatic voice in relation to the line, almost a musical interplay in which the entire form of a completed story becomes audible.

Where Seth's novel owes much to Byron and Pushkin, and Turner's epics to Milton, many contemporary writers of shorter narratives look back upon Robert Frost as the most significant practitioner of their art. Frost's "Home Burial," for example, elucidates two characters and their dramatic conflict in a mere 116 lines. With economy most fiction writers would admire, Frost plunges us into the midst of marital estrangement in his first two lines:

> He saw her from the bottom of the stairs
> Before she saw him. She was starting down....

The first line is a statement of fact, but enjambment forces us into the second line; the line break itself, and the power struggle implicit in the phrase "Before she saw him," creates suspense. He is at the bottom of the stairs, she at the top. But she is coming down, and already we know that their meeting will produce conflict. As the poem progresses, the suspense it achieves by line breaks and withholding exposition pulls us uncomfortably close to these two people. Frost's spare dialogue uses repetition to further suspense, while also capturing the man's alienation from his wife's grief:

> He spoke
> Advancing toward her: "What is it you see
> From up there always?—for I want to know."
> She turned and sank upon her skirts at that,
> And her face changed from terrified to dull.
> He said to gain time: "What is it you see?"

The repeated question indicates the husband's helpless frustration, even trepidation, but he speaks "Advancing toward her"—his gesture is intrusive. She, who had been "Looking over her shoulder at some fear," grows impassive, as if an impenetrable wall stood between them.

Both husband and wife know this wall intimately. He knows it even as he feigns ignorance of what put it there. Her angry grief and his coldness have built it, and though he insists that he will know what troubles her, she nests in her own bitterness, confident that he cannot know her secret. In the first twenty lines of the poem, Frost maps with scary accuracy the dimensions of their estrangement. Their situation is specific. Not only does their dead child's recently-filled grave, which is visible from an upstairs window, haunt her, but her pain is multiplied by the image of her husband digging—even being able to dig. When he speaks about the graves, then about their child's grave, his sensitivity is clumsy:

"There are three stones of slate and one of marble,
Broad-shouldered little slabs there in the sunlight
On the sidehill. We haven't to mind *those*.
But I understand: it is not the stones,
But the child's mound—"

       "Don't, don't, don't,

  don't," she cried.

The verse itself, the husband's full lines wordily groping for explanation and the wife's spondaic outburst finishing a line, contributes powerfully to the scene. Details of psychological states share space in the above passage with a detail of social milieu: as in Dickens, the gravestones almost become characters, telling of the generations of broad-shouldered farmers from whom the husband is apparently descended.

This kind of specific touch is the lifeblood of any good story, but the poet balances even more precariously, dangerously, because of the added technical difficulty of versification. Mark Jarman's dramatic monologue, "The Gift," in his book *The Black Riviera* (1990), uses blank verse as strict as Frost's to limn a specific child's point of view when she is "kidnapped" for a day by her father. As her father drives them in his car, she observes,

Outside the windshield traffic lights hung down
From cables, and the bushy tops of palms
Showed up at intervals that I could count.
A pink or yellow building front skimmed past.
But mostly I could only see the sky.

By themselves these lines are unremarkable, but in their dramatic context, given the strangeness of the event, her limited point of view and touching pride in being able to count, they carry much of the poem's disjointed mood. When the father's girlfriend shows up, Jarman's careful establishment of the speaker's voice pays off nicely:

Then, at a stop, one of those tall palm trees
That wears a shaggy collar of dead fronds
Leaned down and opened up the door and got in
Beside me. Daddy called her Charlotte dear
And told her I was Susan.

Still, the lines themselves do not quite pay the sort of metrical dividends Frost's do. Most contemporary narrative poets are not yet adept at milking the techniques of enjambment and metrical variation for specific dramatic effects.

Despite this weakness, Jarman has made some of the most ambitious narrative forays of any poet of his generation. In "The Death of God" he experiments with the long free verse line of Robinson Jeffers, a line that enables Jarman in his next book, *Iris* (1992), the freedom and sweep of a novelist:

> The woman sat on the bus, her daughter's head in her lap,
> > and read a paperback of poems,
> The only book from college that she'd saved, Robinson
> > Jeffers, and talked back to him,
> As always. He was her poet. The bus crossed the two
> > lakes, and the land between them,
> Like stages of warning. Glare of water, shadow of close,
> > dense trees, glare again.
> Then entry into the isolated flatland that she'd left,
> > married, pregnant, unhurt,
> Not yet in thrall to this dead stranger from California,
> > who spoke of an end to the continent
> She had to imagine, had to summon up even more
> > strenuously while coming back
> To western Kentucky, a mother, estranged, abused and
> > wounded, hiding a black-eye behind dark glasses.

Jarman's protagonist, a woman torn between the decadent reality of contemporary life and the transcendent vision of Jeffers' ghost, begins a quest that Jarman the novelist cannot quite resolve; the book's lyrical resolution synthesizes sound, meaning and event as only a poet could do. Indeed, if much of *Iris* has the feel of a prose novel, its conclusion almost escapes plot altogether with its lyrical loft.

Like Jarman, Robert McDowell has brought a rugged idiom and subject matter to his poetry. His first book, *Quiet Money* (1987), works by a kind of narrative architecture as much as by the devices of a poet. In blank and free verse poems, one finds here a world akin to Raymond Carver's, in which failure predominates. The title poem, about a bootlegging pilot who has made secret transatlantic flights for years before Lindbergh's famous one, becomes one of several lovely meditations on the salvation of skill and craft. It also proves beyond any doubt that real stories have indelible structures. They are like seeds containing blueprints of complex entities, and keep growing in the mind long after one has read them. Since *Quiet Money*, McDowell has published, mostly in *The Hudson Review*, more narratives with a gritty urban vision one rarely finds in poetry, particularly "The Neighborhood," "My Corporate Life" and "All the Broken Boys and Girls." These are poems in which McDowell's blank verse technique seems increasingly assured. One of the strongest of his recent poems, "The Pact," proves a dark pastoral tale combining the narrative obsession of Jeffers with the verse technique of Frost. Its vivid opening reads as follows:

> Rain bulled into the valley like a giant
> Escaping from the pages of a book.
> John-Allen in his garden watched it brawling
> Over the coastal range. Its highest peaks
> Gleamed briefly in the sun that broke above
> The Cascade Mountains fifty miles to the east,
> Then disappeared in swirling thunderheads.
> Behind him his blue house reflected deeper blue
> As all the valley darkened. He leaned the rake
> Against the cockeyed table of surplus boards
> And walked back to the fence to face the wind
> Coming in warm gusts that flattened the grass,
> Advanced on the pear tree, then on himself.
> His straw hat blew off, flew crazily away,
> Splitting the wicket of two apple trees
> Before hanging up suddenly among the roses.
> John-Allen still faced west, his hair straight back,
> His eyes tearing. He knew he should go in
> But tightened his grip on the fence. The storm inside
> Would outlast this one, which was beautiful.
> A moment's silence, then thunder came calling,
> Then all the fury of the storm broke loose.

In clean, skillfully-modulated lines, McDowell establishes his setting and the ominous potential of "the storm inside." "The Pact" achieves a powerful marriage of story and line. More recently, McDowell has published his own book-length poem, *The Diviners*, which demonstrates yet again another of his specific skills: the management of third-person narration—something no other New Narrative poet has brought off with as much consistent success.

Due to Frost's influence on these contemporary poets, it seems appropriate here to note Mary Jo Salter's sympathetic biography in verse, "Frost at Midnight." Here she retells stories familiar from prose biographies, but with an economy and cumulative power that honor her subject:

> Now Frost is eighty-eight. He can see ahead.
> Poet of chance and choice, who tossed a coin
> but knew which side his bread was buttered on,
> who said, "The most inalienable right of man
> is to go to hell in his own way, "here he is
> in a hospital bed, a hell he hasn't made.
> He has a letter from Lesley, who knows him for
> the stubborn vanities and selfless gestures.
> She knows, dear girl, the words to make him well,
> if anything can make him well. She calls him
> "Robert Coeur de Lion." Too weak to write,
> he dictates a final letter back to her.
> "You're something of a Lesley de Lion
> yourself," he says, and he commends the children's
> poems she's been working on. It's good
> to have a way with the young. The old man
> hasn't lost his knack, even in prose,
> for giving truth the grandeur of a cadence.
> "I'd rather be taken for brave than anything else."

Salter captures the sad humor and durability of a man who put what faith he had into his art, but like a good fiction writer she also allows us to feel the weight, as it were, of a specific life.

The saddest moment in Frost's "Home Burial" occurs when the wife, who has been almost menacingly silent, suddenly and at length describes her husband's grave-digging. Here the verse itself is compelled by the extremity of contained emotion:

"...you don't know how to speak.
If you had any feelings, you that dug
With your own hand—how could you?—his little grave;
I saw you from that very window there,
Making the gravel leap and leap in air,
Leap up, like that, like that, and land so lightly
And roll back down the mound beside the hole.
I thought, Who is that man? I didn't know you.
And I crept down the stairs and up the stairs
To look again, and still your spade kept lifting."

Now, the wife's resentment given voice, it is the husband's turn to
withdraw in bitterness, his brevity proving that language cannot
bridge the gulf between them: "I shall laugh the worst laugh I ever
laughed. / I'm cursed. God, if I don't believe I'm cursed."

Though Frost's use of the line for dramatic effect is more successful than any of his imitators', his diction is sometimes awk-
ward, as when the husband says, "I don't like such things 'twixt
those that love." Narrative poets are caught between the lyric possibilities of the line and the necessities of storytelling, and occasionally one or the other of these elements suffers. Two of the most
remarkable recent dramatic monologues, Dana Gioia's "The Room
Upstairs" (from *Daily Horoscope*, 1986) and "Counting the Children"
(The Gods of Winter, 1991), blend lyric and dramatic elements almost seamlessly. Gioia's tactic is usually to be as unobtrusive as
possible, and in both of these poems he chooses speakers well-suited
to his clear, meticulous voice and probing intelligence. This is particularly true of "Counting the Children," in which the speaker is,
as Gioia once was, a businessman. Beyond that fact we know little
about Mr. Choi, a Chinese-American accountant hired to audit the
estate of an eccentric old woman who has recently died. We do not
see him interacting with other characters, as we do the husband
and wife in Frost's more dramatic poem. We hear a neighbor woman
speaking as she shows Mr. Choi through the house, but he does
not respond vocally to anything she says. Gioia limits the poem to
the confines of Choi's mind, so it resembles a private confession to
the reader. Because of this, Gioia's lines are not used dramatically
in the manner of Frost; they are rarely broken out of narrative
necessity, but instead retain a fluid, dream-like suppleness. Gioia's

poem lacks Frost's firm grounding in a specific milieu; instead, like Poe, he emphasizes the subjective view, linking Mr. Choi's fevered vision to lyric moments in the verse.

No great drama propels this vision. Touring the house, Mr. Choi has been shown the dead woman's strange collection of dolls. His function among them is purely professional and legalistic, but the roomful of dolls on shelves startles him out of his routine:

> Where were the children who promised them love?
> The small, caressing hands, the lips which whispered
> Secrets in the dark? Once they were woken,
>
> Each by name. Now they have become each other—
> Anonymous except for injury,
> The beautiful and headless side by side.

These are well-written lines, but the image of "The beautiful and headless side by side" does more to develop a mood than to illuminate Mr. Choi's character. Still, Gioia has pulled us into a mind that is recognizably individual. In the second section of "Counting the Children" Choi has a nightmare in which he cannot balance his ledger; his world has lost its customary order, and even numbers disobey him. The madness of that doll collection, of a mind that could assemble so many dead pairs of eyes, so many frozen little corpses, suggests a whole world unhinged, and when, in the third section, Choi awakes, his first thought is for his daughter's safety. He gropes down the hallway to her room, discovering her safely asleep. Gioia may have felt that the following openly emotional lines could not be written without the protective mask of a dramatic monologue:

> How delicate this vessel in our care,
> This gentle soul we summoned to the world,
> A life we treasured but could not protect.
>
> This was the terror I could not confess—
> Not even to my wife—and it was the joy
> My daughter had no words to understand.

> So standing at my pointless watch each night
> In the bare nursery we had improvised,
> I learned the loneliness that we call love.

Too pretty, some might say, yet in a manner that is quite unlike Frost's, Gioia has risked feelings of uncommon delicacy.

If we scarcely know Mr. Choi as a social being, it is also true that Gioia uses the man's profession, a life of columned numbers, to make specific psychological observations about dream and reality, introducing us to a world and a mind seldom seen in contemporary poetry. "And though you won't believe that an accountant/ Can have a vision," he says, "I will tell you mine." The man's powerful need to shift into visionary experience, dramatized in his protective feelings for his daughter, is matched by Gioia's lyrical lines:

> We long for immortality, a soul
> To rise up flaming from the body's dust.
> I know that it exists. I felt it there,
>
> Perfect and eternal in the way
> That only numbers are, intangible but real,
> Infinitely divisible yet whole.

Here the visionary sense (a restrained and muted version of what we sometimes find in Jeffers) opens the cage of the narrative, allowing the secret it contained to fly. Frost's vision is darkly realistic, Gioia's at first more hopeful, but the last image in Gioia's poem is of the daughter's lifeless dolls, their eerie faces challenging Mr. Choi's assertions. Gioia pulls us into a dramatized epiphany that teaches us about human yearning the way Frost teaches us about grief, and he does this without seeming high-handed or condescending.

The best narrative poems instruct us about life, but also about poetic practice. There must be some reason why the story had to be told in lines, some advantage to the line as a unit that is actually used by the poet to achieve effects possible by no other means. Frost's use of line breaks is a good example of this. In some cases, the lyric qualities of the line lend the narrative cohesion; the climax or crux of the story is also a climax of sound, a moment in which saying finds an extraordinary rightness, an inevitability, as it does in Gioia's "Counting the Children." Prosaic and lyric moments will undoubtedly alternate in even the best dramatic poems, and the prosaic will leave them vulnerable to the charge that what is written is not poetry. That is why there must be, at some key point or points, a benefit from the use of lines. Good narratives have been written in free verse as well as meter, but in the best of these poems there is always a moment when we know we are hearing poetry, not prose, when the line transforms thought, feeling, plot and character into memorable speech. This needn't always be a moment of high sensuousness. Frost recalls laughing with Ezra Pound over the following lines from a short poem by Edwin Arlington Robinson:

> Miniver scorned the gold he sought,
>   But sore annoyed was he without it;
> Miniver thought, and thought, and thought,
>   And thought about it.

As Frost points out, the final "thought," so telling of Miniver's character, achieves its charm by being placed in another line. The line break and the shift from tetrameter to dimeter verse contribute to precision of effect.

Whatever narrative voice is used — first, second or third person — the storyteller faces a dilemma of style. In dramatic poems, rhythm and diction are not wholly governed by the poet's predilections. Rather, the poet negotiates with character, and this negotiated voice must be one in which neither poet nor character is compromised. Prose stylists have the same problem, exacerbated by our modern reliance on realism. Henry James's sentences, so adept at capturing the nuances of adult minds, fail to accommodate the child's in *What Maisie Knew.* It is too easy for the stylist to condescend to his or her subject and thereby hold at a distance what ought to be intimate knowledge. The storyteller's ego must share the stage with others. Jarman and McDowell use the diction of characters from a variety of backgrounds, while Gioia chooses speakers capable of his fluid lyricism. In either approach the poet balances on a very thin line. We don't want our stories told by nonentities, but we want even less for the characters to become nonentities. We want those other lives in their particularity, otherwise we cannot believe in them as lives. At the beginning of his short story, "The Rich Boy," F. Scott Fitzgerald writes, "Begin with an individual, and before you know it you find that you have created a type; begin with a type, and you find that you have created—nothing."

Finally, narrative and dramatic poems are often at some level personal. This is the paradox of the mask, the persona: it liberates the personal by objectifying it. A male poet may write about a middle-aged woman whose father committed suicide when she was very young, and who, as a result, has never had the opportunity to feel young herself; the poet's narrative may be fueled, as it were, by his own anxieties and neuroses stemming from family problems and their effects upon children. His father has not committed suicide, but his parents were divorced and left him feeling helpless and prematurely aged. He tells her story because he can see hers clearly, his vision unclouded by self-pity. But he too is implicated; no audience would care to listen if he weren't. I have no doubt that the death of Frost's three-year-old son gave "Home Burial" some of its accuracy and power, just as the death of Gioia's infant son gave emotional truth to the meditations of "Counting the Children."

Poetic lines remain a viable medium for characterization as well as narrative, and the necessities of fiction may contribute much of value to the poet's work, making it accessible beyond a purely literary audience. At a time when so many poets work in the university, when the very architecture of campuses sets them apart from the surrounding communities, and poets encounter an increasingly limited and specialized range of experiences, narrative poems offer the unexplored territory of other lives. Poets may write about farmers or business people, children or terrorists; the point is that they look into the larger community, into the hearts of strangers, helping to restore the relation between poetry and the increasingly complicated world.

THE TENACITY OF JOHN HAINES

Nothing stains like blood,
nothing whitens like snow.
   — "In the Forest Without Leaves"

Literary criticism has not yet come to terms with the poetry of America's western coast, and the reasons for this are complex. To begin with, most poets born on the coast, from Robert Frost to Gjertrud Schnackenberg, have been more closely associated with the east and its centers of literary power, Boston and New York. The best-known modern west coast poets who come to mind — Robinson Jeffers, Theodore Roethke, William Stafford and John Haines — were all transplanted from other locales (though Haines spent some important childhood years in California). One can fairly say that these poets *chose* the relative remoteness of their landscapes for private reasons, and, especially in the cases of Jeffers and Haines, forged relatively independent lives out of that remoteness.

Other transplanted poets of note include Kenneth Rexroth, Yvor Winters, Janet Lewis, Thom Gunn, Edgar Bowers, David Wagoner, Suzanne J. Doyle and Timothy Steele; to the list of those born on or near the coast I would add Richard Hugo, Gary Snyder, Carolyn Kizer, Dana Gioia and Robert McDowell. No doubt these lists are woefully incomplete, but perhaps this is symptomatic of the lack of critical consensus about west coast writers. I raise these issues in order to suggest one context in which the career of John Haines can be considered. The publication of his collected poems, *The Owl in the Mask of the Dreamer,* and *Fables and Distances: New and Selected Essays,* as well as *The Wilderness of Vision,* a volume of essays about Haines, provides me with an occasion to outline that career, reflecting not only on its singularity but also on its relation to a part of the world rarely mentioned in our criticism. Having said that, I should add that the burden of Haines' recent writing transcends the limits of regionalism, as all significant writing must. Haines began as a nature poet, but has developed into a poet of significant intellectual range, whose principal subject is the place of the human in nature — of spiritual relations embodied in experience.

Born in 1924 to a somewhat nomadic military family, Haines first went to Alaska after naval service in World War II. Unlike a few other poets of his generation, he has not written directly about the war, but such bitter experience surely underlies his basic mistrust of dominant cultural institutions. After establishing his homestead on 160 acres of land southeast of Fairbanks, he left to continue art studies in Washington D.C. and New York. When he returned to the homestead in 1954, he lived by hunting, trapping and foraging—a period he has beautifully described in his memoirs, *Living Off the Country* and *The Stars, The Snow, The Fire.* He has since traded that subsistence life for the equally precarious one of a freelance writer and itinerant teacher. Few modern poets have been so committed to a life outside the conventional economy— few have been willing to take such extraordinary risks. Nothing could be further from the smug centers of literary power, yet Haines has fashioned a body of work that readers and literary historians cannot entirely neglect. He has even achieved the kind of success signified by literary prizes. More importantly, he has given us a genuinely northwestern sensibility, a voice that, at its best, is mythopoeic while resisting the easy mythology of popular culture— no small achievement for a man who published his first collection at the age of 42.

Despite this late flowering, Haines seems from the start to have taken seriously—perhaps too seriously—the artist's vocation. One notices, for example, a paucity of humor in his work, a lack of ornament, almost a painful sobriety. In at least one of his essays he seems aware of his own formal limitations, writing, "The practice of free verse, as we mostly know it, leaves little choice as to a suitable form, and consequently our poems all tend to look alike and sound alike." If one comes to poetry seeking *memorable* speech, Haines' poems often do little to assist the memory. One doesn't find the luminous rightness of line and diction available in the best work of Richard Wilbur, for example, and some critics have found it easy to dismiss Haines, incorrectly, as an untutored artist. The pleasures of Haines' verse may not be immediately evident to all readers, but they do exist. As Dana Gioia wisely wrote in his preface to *New Poems: 1980-88*, "Haines' poetry speaks best to someone who appreciates the deep solitude out of which art arises. The attention they [sic] require is not so much intellectual as spiritual. To approach this kind of poetry one must trust it, a difficult gesture in an era like ours where so much art is characterized by pretense and vapidity."

The poems of Haines' first book, *Winter News* (1966), remind me of the fluid simplicity of Robert Bly's early work. Here, for example, is "Poem of the Forgotten":

> I came to this place,
> a young man green and lonely.
>
> Well quit of the world,
> I framed a house of moss and timber,
> called it a home,
> and sat in the warm evenings
> singing to myself as a man sings
> when he knows there is no one to hear.
>
> I make my bed under the shadow
> of leaves, and awake
> in the first snow of autumn,
> filled with silence.

One cannot imagine the average New Yorker (if there is such a creature) having much patience with that silence. Perhaps it is an experience available only to those who already know it, the immense silence of a world in which no machines grate and no human voice other than your own fills the void. Even my use of the word "void" is insufficient, because one learns, eventually, how full of life that absence of humanity can be. (I should add, however, that certain New York periodicals like The *Hudson Review* have long supported Haines' work; perhaps his appeal has always been broader than I suggest.)[1]

In the midst of such silence, Haines composed some charming and ambiguous poems. Here is "To Turn Back":

> The grass people bow
> their heads before the wind.
>
> How would it be
> to stand among them, bending
> our heads like that...?

Yes.. and no... perhaps...
lifting our dusty faces
as if we were waiting for
the rain...?

The grass people stand
all year, patient and obedient—

to be among them
is to have only simple
and friendly thoughts,
and not be afraid.

The poem charms me with the unexpected satire of its metaphor; it has the sort of broad appeal I alluded to earlier.

If the poems in *Winter News* derive largely from his homesteading experience, from being in nature, Haines' second book, *The Stone Harp* (1971), reminds us as well of his art school years. His purpose here is not always clear. I do not know what to make, for example, of the final image in "Dürer's Vision":

The country is not named,
but it looks like home.

A scarred pasture,
thick columns of rain,
or smoke...

A dark, inverted mushroom
growing from the sky
into the earth.

Without recourse to a specific illustration, the poem seems only vaguely apocalyptic, one of Haines' weaker efforts. I get more from "The Hermitage" (which is not about an art museum), collected in *Twenty Poems:*

In the forest below the stairs
I have a secret home,
my name is carved in the roots.

I own a crevice stuffed with moss
and a couch of lemming fur;
I sit and listen to the music
of water dripping on a distant stone,
or I sing to myself
of stealth and loneliness.

No one comes to see me,
but I hear outside
the scratching of claws,
the warm, inquisitive breath...

And once in a strange silence
I felt quite close
to the beating of a human heart.

Here the forest found earlier in *Winter News* has again taken on allegorical meaning, as it does in Dante. That "scratching of claws" could refer to a sound the homesteader heard in his silent cabin, but the poem transcends autobiography. Its sense of isolation is more universal than that which most of the earlier poems achieve.

By 1971, when he published *The Stone Harp* and *Twenty Poems*, Haines had established a distinctive free verse technique and a range of subject matter that, for all their successes, still allowed some critics to marginalize or neglect him. Here it might be useful to quote from a letter that William Carlos Williams wrote to Haines on April 21, 1953. "The thing that makes you stand out as a poet," the doctor wrote, "is your unaffected sense of rhythm and your intelligent sense of how to make it an organic part of your composition. In the next paragraph Williams added, "Measure is the secret of that advance (how to measure your verse without strain) SO THAT YOU CAN CONTROL IT consciously and with ease. Instinct is not enough for the master of his craft. Free verse is not enough." Reading Haines' poetry one rarely forgets that one is in the hands of a craftsman, a *makar*, as the Scots call their poets. *Cicada* (1977) and his volume of new and selected poems, *News from the Glacier* (1982), won him new readers, but did little to alter his reputation as a regional writer whose region was far removed from most people's lives. He was poetry's token Alaskan.

With the publication of *New Poems: 1980-88,* Haines revealed larger ambitions. Very little in the book directly reflects his Alaskan experience; instead, he has fashioned longer sequences of meditative lyrics (something he had begun to do in his previous collection). Having established a good but limited range, Haines now steps off into fascinating visionary territory; the silence of his early work becomes the silence in which all human endeavor occurs, as in the beginning of "Days of Edward Hopper":

> These are the houses that stand,
> broken and entered; these
> are the walls written by rain,
> the sparrow arches, the linear
> stain of all that will one day
> turn to smoke in the mind.

I read these newer sequences surprised by a cumulative power I do not fully understand. This meditativeness is not simple-minded, but rigorously earned. What appeared to be naiveté in some of Haines' early poems now becomes harrowing allegory, especially in his concluding sequence, "In the Forest Without Leaves." Here Haines tackles nothing less than the modern ecology, the precarious place of the human in nature. As if to prove to his readers how difficult it has been to develop and sustain this vision, Haines now dates the composition of his poems, some of which have evolved over decades. I find the practice mildly irritating, as if the poet were overly concerned with posterity, but Haines may have felt the need to counteract erroneous perceptions that his writing was effortless.

Images from science, philosophy and art dominate the recent work, yet one of my favorite sequences in *New Poems* is "Rain Country," which moves me with its memories of specific people — Campbell and Peg and Bitter Melvin — who rejected the culture of the Lower 48 and the kinds of political power that still outrage the poet. Yet these durable characters have also gone away or died:

> I write this down
> in the brown ink of leaves,
> of the changed pastoral
> deepening to mist on my page.

I see in the shadow-pool
beneath my hand a mile
and thirty years beyond
this rain-driven autumn.

All that we loved: a fire
long dampened, the quenched
whispering down of faded
straw and yellowing leaves.

The names and the voices
within them, speak now
for the slow rust of things
that are muttered in sleep.

There is ice on the water
I look through, the steep
rain turning to snow.

I have no comfortable jargon to describe the success of this poem, and my quoting only this final section cannot possibly do justice to it. Haines is utterly in command of his technique here. The few unpatterned rhymes — "now" and "snow," "sleep" and "steep" — quietly suggest life's partly-revealed forms. In the final section of *The Owl in the Mask of the Dreamer,* Haines builds on the strengths of these sequences, which thoroughly overcome the limitations found in some of his individual lyrics.

The two poets mentioned most often in his essays are Robinson Jeffers and Edwin Muir, both of whom were born in 1887. They would appear to have little else in common. Contrast Jeffers' prosperous Pittsburgh upbringing and top drawer schooling to Muir's stark Orkney boyhood and poverty in Glasgow. Jeffers moved from the city to his stone tower at Carmel, Muir from islands to grinding slums, finally escaping through education, starting to write poems at 35, translating Kafka with his wife, and capping his career with *The Estate of Poetry,* his wonderful lectures delivered at Harvard. Both poets, however, developed mythic imaginations, describing human experience in classical and biblical terms. Both wrote powerfully about nature. Both assumed an audience of intelligent people who were not necessarily professors; perhaps in consequence, both have been neglected since their deaths by the sort of university-based critic who prefers the unreadable. In terms of their individualism, even their fundamental dourness, one can readily see their influence upon Haines. Perhaps he never developed Muir's example of writing in rhyme and meter because he began to write at a time when free verse still seemed liberating, rather than another kind of rote performance. I don't know. With regard to form, Haines' ideas appear to be both severe and catholic. As he says in one of the essays, "Great poetry has been written in formal measures and strict forms, in 'free' verse, and sometimes as intensified prose. I see no reason why this should not continue to be the case, unless we are going to insist on one or more kinds of orthodoxy and turn the entire thing into a subdivision of politics."

If comparison to Muir points up one kind of shortcoming in Haines' writing, a wholesale neglect of the folk tradition so important to the best Scottish writing, comparison to Jeffers indicates another. Haines' essay on Jeffers is one of the best pieces collected in *Fables and Distances*, revealing that Haines was long aware of the older poet and even made a pilgrimage to Carmel, though he avoided meeting Jeffers out of respect for his privacy. Haines notes that the commercial development of Carmel (something he would later observe in Alaska) never appears in Jeffers' poetry; an artist is more, much more, than a recorder of his environment. An artist must have both strong vision and strong technique, and Haines notes a rare quality in Jeffers' voice:

> When we read a poem these days we take it for granted that the poet is speaking to himself, to another poet, or to an audience of poetry readers or teachers of poetry. I don't say this is necessarily wrong, but it does place very definite limitations on the poetry. We have, for one thing, forgotten how to write in any voice but our own. We miss, I think, the dramatic voice that can only be used in the presence of an audience, actual or imagined. It would be difficult to name any major poet in whom this dramatic voice was entirely absent. ... For Jeffers this sense of the audience was not only instinctive, it was, I think, essential to his poetry. We can never forget while reading him that he is speaking to a certain largeness in us, as to a congregation; his voice, at once personal and public, has that authority.

Though Haines has conceived some poems in voices other than his own ("In the Sleep of Reason" is an example), he is not really a dramatic poet. His larger sequences are meditative; character and narrative play a rather small role in them.

To be fair, he seems alive to these limitations, and the essays impress me again and again with the uncanonical breadth of his affections as a reader. He can also be severe. I, for one, rejoice in his dismissal of John Ashbery's *Hotel Lautreamont*. Haines could have become a hermit and written ever more hermetic verses in the manner of "Dürer's Vision"; instead he has decided to engage the larger world of ideas and political issues, to write as if writing mattered. I sometimes sense a too easy romanticism in his politics, as if it were self-evident that poetry should be subversive. His praise of Carolyn Forché is so vague that I am not sure exactly where he stands with regard to her deeper aesthetic values, especially the nagging sense that her politics are a kind of self-aggrandizement.[2] And in his review of *Expansive Poetry*, a deeply flawed and premature attempt to define the New Formalism, Haines sometimes confuses concern for poetry's audience with careerism, grabbing some awfully high ground for himself:

> ...poetry is not in any useful sense a profession, and it is certainly not a competition, no matter what the behavior of individual poets might at times seem to indicate. It is something else: a complication of reality, a questioning of values and appearances, subversive to the extent that it asks necessary questions; a surrender, a dedication, as well as being at certain times and in certain instances a sacrifice—in which situation all questions as to career and professionalism become irrelevant.

I have already indicated that I believe John Haines when he talks about sacrifice, but plenty of poets leading more conventional lives have also made sacrifices for their art. The kind of poetry Haines describes here, albeit broadly, may be a summit tossed by *Sturm und Drang*, but it hardly represents the range of what is possible or desirable in verse. Passages like this go a long way toward explaining the absence of humor in his collected poems.

That same severity of character limits his charm as a literary memoirist. When at the end of "Within the Words: An Apprenticeship," he reveals that he knew Weldon Kees, Franz Kline, Willem de Kooning and other New York artists, he gives us no anecdotes, no impressions of their personalities, as if mere mention of their names were sufficient. I commend his avoidance of cheap gossip, but the best raconteurs are interested at least partly in characters other than themselves.

These objections aside, I find *Fables and Distances* a rewarding book. He begins his preface by saying, "I have never felt it necessary or appropriate that a poet be limited to writing about poetry." One senses throughout the book a mind weighing ideas against experience, like a skilled carpenter eyeing fresh lumber. He sees the limits of human life, human knowledge, placing what faith he has in nature. Perhaps he would agree with the Irish poet, Derek Mahon, who has written,

> An ordinary common-or-garden brick wall, the kind
> For talking to or banging your head on,
> Resents your politics and bad draughtsmanship.
> God is alive and lives under a stone.
> Already in a lost hub-cap is conceived
> The ideal society which will replace our own.

Haines' aesthetics derive, as any truly valuable aesthetics must, from the meeting places of life and art. He suggests that ultimately the greatest artificer is the one we know least about:

> There is a form that exists, independent of our will and invention, and one need not believe in either God or Plato to acknowledge a truth in this claim. To the extent that a poem corresponds in some degree to this living, timeless, but never more than partly revealed form, the poem will justify itself and outlive its moment of conception. We will call it apt, or fitting, or beautiful, like a house to be lived in.

Haines also writes splendidly about nature and nature writers like John Muir, showing a passionate and justifiable sense of ecological responsibility. Those of us who have even briefly glimpsed real wilderness can't help despairing when we see it whittled — or bulldozed — away. The millions who love the Northwest's beauty have all but destroyed it. Alpine meadows I camped beside as a boy now have to be guarded against trampling crowds, their delicate plants treated almost like works of art behind bullet-proof glass. It is sad and necessary and necessarily sad. Haines' anger about the indiscriminate commercial development of Alaska gives way, or partly gives way, to his recognition of the essential reality of change. It seems fitting that *Fables and Distances*, concludes with a bittersweet memoir about his lost childhood loves.

For readers who discover John Haines' work and want some guidance in reading him, *The Wilderness of Vision* is the best available book. It contains good essays by its editors, Kevin Bezner and Kevin Walzer, as well as appreciations by other poets: Wendell Berry, Don Bogen, Dennis Sampson, Sam Hamill, Dana Gioia and Donald Hall. Don Bogen's essay on the later poems is an especially useful extension of the impression (which I share) of Haines' fundamental romanticism: "Haines' work since 1980 has been an attempt to reconcile his Wordsworthian vision with an increasingly pessimistic view of the world." In his lucid readings, Bogen describes Haines' "drive to find an authentic vision in the face of cosmic annihilation...." Among the reviews reprinted here, Robert Richman's is particularly eloquent and just. Anthony Hecht, in a *Hudson Review* chronicle, responsibly clarifies his own aesthetic grounds for finding defects in *Winter News*. A much more dismissive review is Peter Stitt's of *Cicada*—a review that mixes critical justice with comments I find shockingly inappropriate, like the following:

> This attitude of breathless reverence at times calls to mind the group with which Haines is most generally classed—the Northwest school. The Northwest poets love Indians even more than the rest of us do, of course, and write lots of poems about their mystique.

Here Stitt is the worst sort of snob, revealing his ignorance by dismissing subjects he apparently knows nothing about; his attitude toward the region is a common one. "These people are too naive," the eastern critic seems to say, "too much in love with their vast tracts of empty land in which nothing useful or beautiful has been said." While it is true that Haines can on occasion seem the vaguest sort of mystic or animist, the truth is that a kind of animism underlies much American culture, and for good reason. We are, after all, a country in which wilderness has until recently been a real presence in peoples' lives — a fact that those who have known only domesticated landscapes cannot understand unless they use their imaginations.

The Wilderness of Vision also contains a good interview in which Haines discusses his intuitive approach to composition, which began as an effort "to pare down my eloquence." It would seem a strange example to set before younger poets, this mode of negation, so spare in its affirmations. Perhaps some poets serve less as models for others than as examples of singular achievement. Perhaps Haines is, in both his life and his work, inimitable. As he writes in *Fables and Distances*, "Poetry, the making of the poem, is an act whose significance we can only grasp through the force of a great example; without that we have no measure." Haines has set his example before us. He has brought a few extraordinary landscapes into American literature, and, more importantly, he has given us the acute attention of a shaping mind.

[1] In a letter to me, Haines has recently written that he feels his work has often been well-received in the east, noting the success of *News from the Glacier* in particular. It may be that, as a westerner myself, I have overstated the prejudices of eastern critics. Indeed, it sometimes seems that the west hardly notices its poets.

[2] Haines has greatly clarified his position on political poetry in an interview published in *Quarter After Eight* (Ohio University, Summer 1996).